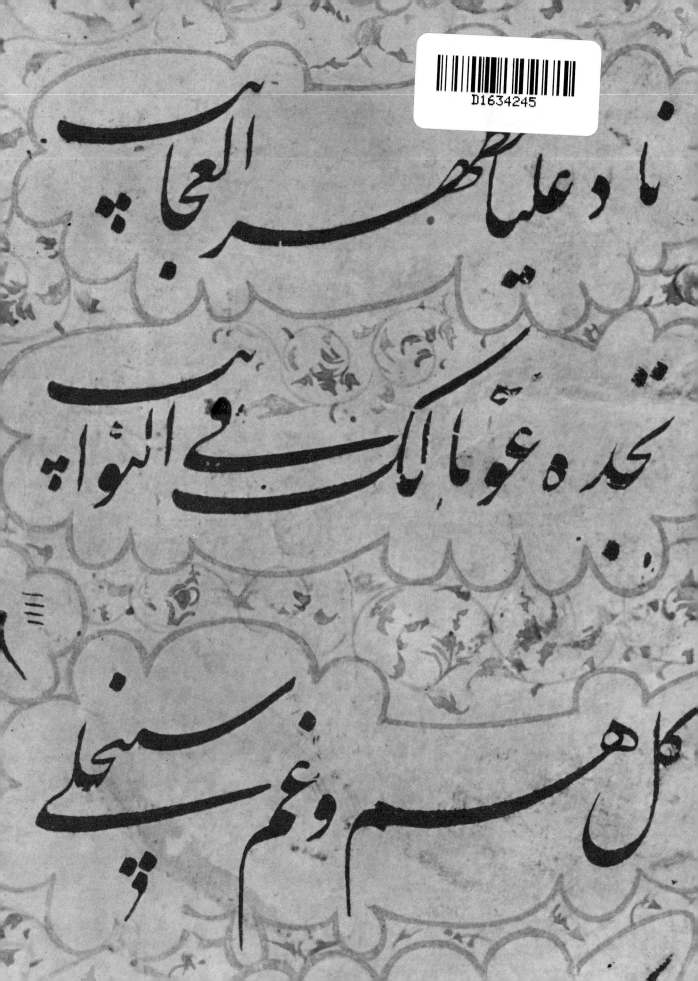

A SPRING ART BOOK

INDIAN MINIATURES
OF THE MOGHUL SCHOOL

Text by
Lubor Hájek

Photographs by
W. and B. Forman

Indian Miniatures
of the Moghul School

Spring Books
London

INDIAN MINIATURES
OF THE MOGHUL SCHOOL

DESIGNED AND PRODUCED BY ARTIA FOR
SPRING BOOKS
SPRING HOUSE · SPRING PLACE · LONDON NW5
© 1960 BY ARTIA PRAGUE
S 832

CONTENTS

INTRODUCTION

The history of Islam begins in 622 A. D. with the Hejira, when Muhammad the Prophet left Mecca for Medina. The creed spread rapidly and only ninety years later we find it knocking at the gates of India. Muhammad Kasim invaded Sind in 712.

A contemporary chronicler records that a group of Hindu painters approached Muhammad Kasim to seek permission to paint his portrait and those of his officers. The chronicle, however, does not say whether the request was granted. One thing, however, is certain, and that is that Kasim and his successors never became patrons of Indian painting.

During the 7th century this art had produced some of the world's finest paintings in the cave temples of Ajanta, and at the time of Kasim's invasion still enjoyed a certain amount of patronage in some parts of India. But in the north-west, occupied by Moslems, its position became precarious. The Turkish rulers of Ghazni who invaded India around 1000 A. D., as well as their conquerors, the Afghans, who in 1192 took Delhi and then gradually overran almost the whole of the country, make their appearance in Indian history as iconoclasts rather than as patrons of the arts. Now and again, of course, cases are recorded of some of them patronising painting, but these are rare and hardly seem to be borne out by the surviving works.

At the end of the 14th century, northern India was invaded by the hordes of the Turko-Mongolian conqueror, Timur, or Tamerlane, the ancestor of the later Mughal Emperors. His stay in this part of the world was brief, but it was enough to show that his attitude towards Indian art was no more

9

enlightened, and, if anything, rather less so, than that of his predecessors.

Such a record was hardly promising, and it must have caused some surprise in the India of the 16th century when, under a new dynasty of Moslem conquerors and rulers, the Mughals, native painting suddenly burst out in a new, rich flower. If we look back over the history of Indian art, we see a barren desert of nearly a thousand years intervening between the peaks of the seventh century Ajanta art and the rise of the Mughal miniature. This sudden appearance of Mughal art, therefore, must be considered surprising. How did it happen?

The answer is that art does not just 'happen'. The history of Mughal art shows this. There is no country or era completely lacking in gifted individuals. All that is necessary is to find them and to give them encouragement and security. In ten years' time the studios will be full of painters; in another ten, their work will have developed a native style with its own artistic laws.

Of course, the growth of Mughal art was not as simple as this, but, in essence, it remains true that it was the product of Imperial patronage. It took some thirty or forty years for it to take root, and after further years of careful tending it grew into a plant of such toughness that it was able to withstand the vicissitudes of two hundred years of Indian history, to put out offshoots, and, simply, to survive.

One of the first Europeans to appreciate Mughal art was Rembrandt. He had a collection of miniatures and, according to his historians, Lugt and Benesch, Mughal influence may be seen in two of his drawings executed around 1638, and in some twenty later works (between 1650 and 1656). And he, no doubt, was not alone. His contemporary and fellow-

10

countryman, Schellinks, for instance, painted in the middle of the 17th century a picture that shows clearly a respect for Mughal models, as well as a considerable knowledge of their historical background.

European professional art-historians, on the other hand, showed no awareness of the existence of Mughal art before the present century. Even then, the tendency was to classify it as a provincial offshoot of the Persian miniature. It was not, in fact, until the 1930's that the art achieved proper recognition, thanks largely to the work of Binyon, Stchoukine, Brown, Goetz, Staude and Wilkinson, and of such Indian interpreters as Khandalawala, Mehta and Krishnadasa.

In appraising the Mughal miniatures, we must be careful not to be too dogmatic, since the full extent of the original work is uncertain. If we take into account the low resistance of paper to the Indian climate, as well as the wars that destroyed many Mughal masterpieces composed of stronger materials than paper and pigments, it seems likely that the corpus of Mughal art suffered considerably, more, for instance, than European art over the same period.

A considerable number of the dozens of illustrated manuscripts and thousands of miniatures that have survived has already been published. This present selection consists, in the main, of hitherto unpublished miniatures. They come mostly from the Iranian state collections (into which they probably found their way following Nadir Shah's exploits in 1739), and were lent to Prague for the 1956 Exhibition. They are supplemented by several miniatures belonging to Indian museums, lent to the Exhibition of Indian Art organised in Prague in 1955 by the All-Indian Academy of Art. Finally, there are some folios from Czechoslovak collections.

11

I

All important stages of Mughal painting are represented, although the emphasis is on the period of the art's greatest glory, at the beginning of the 17th century.

My text is not intended as a general introduction to Indian miniatures of the Mughal School, for there are already a number of very good books of this nature (see Bibliography). Instead I have tried to trace the main characteristics of the miniatures and ascertain their relation to the historical background. The reader will find that I use terms normally only met with in linguistic studies — the reason being that I am not sure whether our Western aesthetic vocabulary can adequately express all the features encountered in the Mughal miniature. In this connection, I would like to thank Mr J. V. Neústupný for some useful suggestions. Further, I owe my thanks to Dr. Věra Stivínová and Mr J. Marek of the Prague Oriental Institute.

THE PAINTINGS

The term, 'Mughal miniature', is applied to those paintings that came into being under the patronage of the Mughal Emperors, and to works closely associated with them.

Herman Goetz believes that the Mughal paintings were not the first Moslem art to appear in India, and that they were preceded by other Moslem schools in the 14th and 15th centuries. The evidence for this, however, is mainly literary. Only a few surviving folios may with any certainty be classified as pre-Mughal work. What is certain is that, during the Middle Ages, the native merchants of Gujarat were much greater patrons of painting than the Moslem rulers of India.

14

The Emperor Babur founded the Mughal dynasty in 1526. We know from his memoirs that he admired painting, and particularly the work of the Herat masters, Bihzad and Shah Musavvir. But he had little opportunity to further the art. The remaining four years of his life were spent in unceasing wars with the Afghans and the Rajputs.

These wars were continued by his son, Humayun (1530 — 1556), although with rather less success. In 1540, he was driven out of India by the Indo-Afghan prince, Sher Shah. For a year, he was given asylum by the Persian ruler, Shah Tahmasp, who then helped to establish him in Kabul. It was only towards the end of his life that Humayun regained Delhi where he died the following year.

From his biography, written by his sister, we know that Humayun took an interest in painting while at the Persian court. At his own court in Kabul, he employed two artists, Mir Sayyid Ali of Tabriz and Abdus Samad of Shiraz. These artists are commonly regarded as the founders of the Mughal school. But it is far from certain whether any of the known paintings of this period is the work of one or other of these artists. Some experts claim that Humayun commissioned them in 1550 to illustrate the *Dastan-i-Amir Hamza* manuscript; others that work on the manuscript was not begun until 1567, in the twelfth year of the reign of Humayun's successor, Akbar. The growth of the Mughal school cannot, therefore, be placed with any certainty before 1570.

Akbar came to the throne as a thirteen-year old boy and proceeded, at first with the help of his Regent, Bairam, and later on his own, to strengthen his position in northern India. The struggle was a long one, and he succeeded only step by step. The Imperial *ateliers*, in which the Mughal miniaturists

15

worked, were, it seems, only built after 1570 during a period when the economy and finances of the growing Empire were being re-organized on a sound basis, and which saw the inauguration of a more active building programme (the fortresses of Agra and Fathpur Sikri date from this time).

Of the 125 surviving illustrations to the *Amir Hamza* romance it is doubtful whether more than two were completed before 1570. But regardless of whether the work had been initiated by Akbar or Humayun, the illustrating of this manuscript with 1400 big pictures was an ambitious undertaking, and its realisation became a sort of 'training school for Mughal artists'. It seems obvious that such a task could not have been carried out by Humayun's two painters alone. Many painters were called in from all over India and soon there were hundreds of them engaged in the work.

Dastan-i-Amir Hamza is a popular romance in which the historical figure of Muhammad's uncle becomes the mythical hero of numerous stories and anecdotes. In their illustrations, the Mughal painters equal the lively imagination of the story-tellers by the vividness and exuberance of their pictorial expression. The illustrations are brimming over with action, objects, people, trees and animals. However miraculous the occurrences depicted, they always reflect a sharp eye for the detail of everyday life — the setting is contemporary, the characters wear the clothes of the period.

The illustrations to the *Amir Hamza* romance were finished after fifteen years, in 1582. In the same year, on Akbar's orders, the illustrating of the *Razm-nama*, the Persian translation of the Indian epic, the *Mahabharata*, was begun. This took six years to complete (although it may have continued longer on some versions). The Persian masters seem to have had less

16

say in this work; perhaps they no longer felt it necessary to hold the hand of the Indian painters. Whatever the case, the native Indian style prevails to such an extent that some of the illustrations are reminiscent more of the early work of the Rajput school, than of the Mughal miniature.

All the early illustrations from the Akbar ateliers show the artists at great pains to break away from the influence of both the Persian and medieval Indian styles of painting. This can be clearly seen in the London copy of the *Darab-nama* manuscript, the Munich copy of the *Shah-nama*, and in the version of the *Timur-nama* in the Bankipur Library. The illustrations to each of these works have a marked affinity with one or other of the earlier traditions. At the same time, it is apparent that the Mughal painters are trying out new solutions to the problems of painting. They succeeded in solving these problems by 1590. By then the typical Akbar style had reached maturity and found its fullest expression in the illustration of historical works, the *forte* of the school.

These works included the History of the Persian Kings (*Shah-nama*): The History of Timur (*Timur-nama*): The History of Babur (*Babur-nama*): Rashid-ud-din's History of the Mongols (*Jami-ut-tawarikh*): The History of the World, (*Tarikh-i-Alfi*): and, finally, Akbar's own history as recorded by the Emperor's biographer Abul Fazl (*Akbar-nama*). Of these various manuscripts, five copies of Babur's History have survived (two in London, and one each in Paris, Moscow and New Delhi), two copies of the History of the Mongols (one in Paris, one in Teheran: see Plates 2 to 5), and one copy of Akbar's History (in London). Each of these manuscripts contains dozens of illustrations, all aimed at giving a faithful rendering of the particular event described in the text.

17

Besides historical works, the painters of Akbar's ateliers also illustrated classical Persian literature — *Khamsa* by Nizami, the romantic love-poem of Leila and Majnun, the collections of moral tales by Sadi and Jami, the Persian translation of the Indian fables of Bidpai-Anwar-i-Suhaili. All these illustrated works are now, in one or two copies, in English collections.

Akbar's death in 1605 after a reign of fifty years brought about a change of emphasis in Mughal painting. In the period marked by the reign of his son, Jahangir (1605—27), and grandson, Shah Jahan (1627—58), the illustration of manuscripts became of lesser concern and interest was focussed on the production of pictures for albums. Jahangir was a passionate lover of painting. He organised a staff of excellent painters, supervised their work, and took the best of their miniatures, as well as a variety of other pictures and calligraphies, bound in magnificently adorned albums.

The most beautiful of these albums appears to have been taken to Persia during the 18th century, from where, during the following century, over twenty of its sheets passed *via* the Prussian Ambassador into the possession of the State Gallery in Berlin and into other collections.[1] Another part of the album remained in Persia and is now in the Imperial Library in Teheran (this is known as the Golshan Album: see Plates 8—32). The finest album from the Shah Jahan era, containing 49 miniatures, is now in the Freer Gallery, Washington. A further three albums, assembled during the same period, are today in England. These are the Minto Album, divided between the Chester Beatty Collection and the Victoria and Albert Museum; Johnson's Album in the India Office Library; and, also in the India Office Library, the album presented by the unhappy prince, Dara Shikoh, to his wife. Most of the

18

miniatures of the first part of the 17th century nevertheless remained unbound and were not collected in albums before the end of the century, or during the following century.

Illustrations of classical Persian literature, paintings of historic events, and compositions of an epic character generally, are in a minority in the Jahangir's and Shah Jahan's ateliers. Such paintings as there are, are usually works painted in the afterglow of the Akbar school, or paintings by Persian artists invited by Jahangir to his court (Plates 22—24). The range of events depicted in this period has narrowed to a few important events or festive occasions as: Jahangir's lion-hunting (the miniature by Manohar Das in Moscow and another in Oxford); the encounter of Jahangir's envoy with the Shah of Persia (Boston); Prince Murad's meeting with the Uzbek ruler, Nazar Muhammad (Benares); and Jahangir taking leave of his son, or welcoming him back from an expedition (Boston, India Office).

At this time, the painters became increasingly concerned with the problem of fidelity in portraiture. This led naturally to a switch from mass representation of figures, where the problem lay in the grouping (Plate 41), to pictures with a smaller number of figures, sometimes only one, or paintings of a bust or head (Plates 8, 10, 21, 34, 35). The largest number of portraits depict the Emperor and his sons. Then follow pictures of some of the more important courtiers, for instance those of Asaf Khan and Shah Daulat; of poets, musicians and artists (Illustrations V and VI, Plates 33, 35, 29); of anonymous servants, hunters, astrologers, artisans and the like (Plates 16, 18, 27, 28, 30).

Portraits of women were not uncommon, although not as frequent as in the later Mughal miniatures. The Moslem

19

religion, however, erected a formidable barrier between women and everyday life. Painters would obviously not have been permitted inside the harem, so that they may have had to draw on their own imagination or on the services of prostitutes as models. On the other hand, it is possible that there were women painters who worked inside the harems, or that in this era *purdah* was not so strictly observed. In this case, the portraits would be individual likenesses and not mere idealisations (Plates 7, 37, 40).

The Emperors' wives may have made public appearances, and the portraits of the famous Empresses, Jogdh Bai and Nur Jahan may have been painted from life.

Jahangir's albums are not infrequently adorned with European engravings presented to the Emperor by the Jesuit missionaries of Goa (Plates 8 and 10). Most of these engravings are copies by Dutch mannerists after Dürer, Rottenhammer and Beham. The Mughal painters often copied these engravings, as well as pictures brought as gifts to Jahangir by the British Ambassador, Sir Thomas Roe.

In some cases these copies are exact replicas; in others, there is a looser treatment of themes drawn from Christianity, European classical mythology, portraiture and so on (Plates 31 and 32).

Today, the most widely-appreciated and sought-after works of the Jahangir and Shah Jahan *ateliers* are the pictures of animals, birds and flowers. The painters depicted animals fighting and during hunting expeditions (Plates 27, 28, 39) and also painted actual animal portraits (Plates 10 and 17). Ustad Mansur, Manohar, Muhammad Nadir and others bequeathed to posterity dozens of such paintings of animals and birds from the Imperial menageries and aviaries. In

20

addition, on orders from the Emperor, they painted many rare flowers and trees.

However, with the accession to the throne in the mid-17th century of the orthodox Moslem, Aurangzib (1658 — 1707), the output of the Imperial *ateliers* declined sharply. The Emperor appears only to have tolerated painters as creators of official portraits, but even here he was insensitive to quality and incapable of giving a lead to the *ateliers* as his two predecessors had done. Most of the Mughal miniatures of the second half of the century owe their existence more to the courtiers than the Emperor. The painters turned towards the portrayal of court beauties of the day, although the illustration of the classic subjects of Persian literature was not quite forgotten. Here, though, sentimentality and sensuality crept in, and tended to displace the previous masterly observation and acute feeling for detail.

This, *mutatis mutandis*, is true also of the 18th century, when the Mughal miniature enjoyed two transient revivals, during the first two decades and around 1770 (Plates 46—50), although the second of these, centred round the painter, Mir Kalan Khan at Oudh, was of rather an eclectic character. Many precise copies of earlier miniatures were produced during this period, and we are indebted to it for the survival of many miniatures of the seventeenth century, which were collected and bound in albums together with contemporary works and copies. The Swiss, Polier, assembled many albums between 1767 and 1776. Six of these are now in German collections.

Some of the eighteenth-century miniatures suggest that the art of the miniature was not entirely forgotten at a time when the history of the Empire was one of retreat and disintegration.

21

In the 19th century, the reflex of the art brought into being a trade in ivory trinket-miniatures for the tourist market. But the true Mughal miniature was so interwoven with the political and economic structure of the Empire that it could not hope to survive its fall.

THE AESTHETIC

Let us imagine a picture of a horse, one of Jahangir's favourite horses, perhaps, a picture that pleased him and his courtiers, the artist who painted it, his colleagues of the Imperial *ateliers* (with reservations, naturally!) and, finally, ourselves.

The real horse, the animal endowed with body and life, with thousands of equine characteristics, and, above all, with actual existence, had to undergo a great many metamorphoses before it became transported into the sphere of art in the Mughal miniature. This process is true of all works of art: the artist has to employ a host of clever tricks, distortions, stylizations, and so on, before he is able to produce an image which will convey the reality to his audience. The ways in which he carries out these various distortions become the aesthetic laws of his particular art-form.[2] Thus, if we examine some of the distortions that take place at various stages of Mughal painting, we shall acquire some rough idea of its basic aesthetic principles.

The artist must, first of all, select from the whole range of subjective and objective reality those elements that he intends to use in his work. This initial act of choice, however, is in itself a distortion, for it implies that what is selected has

22

significance. The choise of subject-matter, therefore, is in effect the first interpretative function of an art.

It is this first choice, already, that differentiates the Mughal miniatures from the rest of the Indian paintings. In Indian art generally, possibly because of its predominantly religious character, the symbolic level is always the more important. The depicted surface reality always very strongly implies some general statement. For instance, the animals and plants of the Buddhist frescoes are not just animals and plants but symbols of the whole of creation, a statement that it is animated, that it feels and suffers. The Rajasthani miniature, though historically closely related to the Mughal miniature, is even more obviously burdened with symbolism. A painting of Krishna with a herd of cows carries metaphysical and erotic overtones; a picture of lovers suggests, for example, a musical key and the season of the year.

The Mughal miniature, however, runs counter to this general trend in Indian art. It is non-symbolic; it does not imply any reality that it does not portray. Exceptions to this rule are to be found only on the fringes of the art, for instance in the early *Hamza-nama* illustrations, which lack the robust objectivity of the later works and suggest to us that they are trying to make some moral statement. Similarly, in the closing phases of the miniature, we come across paintings in which there appears to be an unresolved conflict between the surface and underlying levels of communication.

Spiritual and emotional matters never occupied the first place in the Mughal scheme of things. This was filled by a sincere, if rather naïve, interest in the subject-matter itself. We see this characteristic for the first time in Babur's annals, in this skilful and objective accounts of Indian scenes. Akbar's

23

و مرد گان ... روی مشفاق برادرانه ای بو کار نصیحت فرمود وکفت تزا لشکری گران وسپاهی بی پایان از

third son, Daniyal, confesses candidly that for art to interest him it must deal with subjects within his own experience, with something 'that we ourselves have seen and heard'. Jahangir devotes long passages in his memoirs to the description of Indian plants and animals. In his diary he records, over a period of a month or more, an almost scientific description of two hawks from the moment of copulation to the time of the feeding of the fledglings. About a falcon, given to him as a present, he writes, in 1619: 'What am I to write about the beauty and colours of this bird! It has many beautiful black spots on the wings, the back and the sides. It was so unusual that I ordered Ustad Mansur to make a painting of it.' This aesthetic-cum-ornithological interest of the Emperor may be seen in Mansur's surviving pictures of falcons (Prince of Wales Museum, Boston; British Museum. Jahangir's description of the haggard, dying Inayat Khan shows an equal detachment — 'since it was a very exceptional case, I gave orders to the painters to portray him.' (The portrait survives in one sketch and one completed miniature.) It was only natural that the Emperor's interest should be aroused by unusual things and people — by the obese musician, the emaciated ascetic, the black Ethiopian, Malik Ambara, and that the miniatures should reflect this. But even in the representation of everyday life, the emphasis of the miniature was on objectivity, on the need for veracity and for minute and careful study of detail (see Illustration II, Plates 16, 24 and others).

This objectivity is the basic aesthetic standard of the Mughal miniature. It is only contravened in works outside the main-stream of the art or in those of some particularly creative artist. Ustad Mansur's unofficial sketch of three geese, for instance, (*Oosterse Shatten*, Rijksmuseum, Amsterdam, Pl. 50)

26

reveals a warmth of feeling absent from his usual coolly objective style. In the margins of the albums we come across scenes painted with an unexpected wealth of emotion (Plate 29), and portraits that display some insight into character (Illustration V). However, it is worth noting, that a few masterpieces by the great portraitists display a similar insight, as well as a veracity 'worthy of the modern police dossier'.

Similarly, in the numerous cases where, besides verisimilitude, a scene has a touch of atmosphere, we usually find that it is the work of painter of individuality such as Miskina (Plate 5), Govardhan (Camp Scene, Berlin Library) or Bichitr (The Tambura Player). In miniatures with a Persian theme, the fairy-tale atmosphere softens the realism (Plate 23) and in the later miniatures of the 18th century a theatrical sentimentality is sometimes to be found (Plate 50). We find, next, that the miniature tended to concentrate on objects and events rather than on action or narrative, despite its close relation to epic literature. The miniature is not epic. This is true even of the illustrations from Akbar's era. The Mughal painter is a clumsy story-teller (see Plate 3). He does not unfold a story, but rather shows an important event by, so to speak, piling up an agglomeration of nouns and limiting his use of verbs. A characteristic example of this is Basawan's illustration of the commissioning of Master Rashid-ud-din (Plate 4). Nothing happens in the picture, yet everything seems to suggest that an important event is meant to have taken place. In Jahangir's time, the static quality of the paintings and their concentration on the event becomes even more marked. State occasions, durbars, visits to hermits, all turn to stone under the gaze of the Imperial official photographers. The preponderance of portraits, whether of courtiers, animals, flowers, or beauties,

27

in itself testifies to the victory of the noun over the verb.

Another stage in the deformation of reality, unavoidable for the painter, is the reduction of three-dimensional reality to the two dimensions of his medium. Here, he has the choice of either disregarding the problem and confining himself to the two-dimensional plane — as, for instance, in some of the *apabhramsha* paintings or in the early Rajput miniature — or of creating by some means an illusion of volume and space. Of course, the mere superimposition of figures in a two-dimensional picture is in itself a primitive form of illusion, as it tries to create the impression that the figures higher up in the image are further away. This technique consists of tilting the base of the composition through ninety degrees; in other words, some of the details — a brook, a swimming-pool, a carpet — are drawn from the bird's-eye view, and the figures in direct view (see Plate 21). This was the practice in the Persian miniature and in some of the medieval Indian illustrations.

A very ingenious and elaborate method of creating an illusion of depth was used by the painters of the Ajanta murals.[3] In all probability, they took as their starting-point the experiments of the Indian sculptors, who, in their reliefs, tried to suggest space by depicting their figures simultaneously at eye-level and from above. The Buddhist painters improved on this method by making use of, in addition to the direct view (convergent perspective) and the view from above (divergent perspective), the hierarchical perspective, which places the objects depicted in order according to their importance. S. Kramish calls this method 'multiple perspective'. In this type of perspective, the most important part is played by the bird's-eye view. It enables us to see what is happening behind the wall or the rock, and in this way an almost physical

28

line is drawn between the nearer and more distant objects. The cliff or the building pushes certain figures into the foreground, others it makes retreat into 'receptacles', which, seen together, form a system of mutually-connected spaces.

Some day, perhaps, we shall solve the problem of how this technique crossed the gulf of a thousand years to appear almost unchanged in the Mughal miniature. The multiple perspective first appears in the *Hamza-nama* and evolves towards perfection in the illustrations of the Akbar era (see Illustration I, Plates 1, 2, 6). Mughal perspective, however, differs from that in the Ajanta paintings in its use of new technical devices derived from European painting. These are aimed at conveying the impression of a receding background, chiefly at the horizon, by the introduction of the so-called 'distant view' (*vue lointaine* or *dur numa*, see Ill. II) and of aerial perspective (*plein-airisme*, see Plates 2 and 3). Several miniatures of the 17th century, in particular, display the influence of European ideas of perspective. These latter appear chiefly in the lowered horizon but sometimes the diminished details of the 'distant view' are pushed forward from the horizon into the heart of the foreground, so that the principal figure appears in hierarchical perspective, in a kind of Napoleonic situation (Plate 34).

The device of breaking up the picture into a number of small spaces ('receptacles') was used with great success by the Mughal painters. The 'receptacles' were made up of walls, tents, canopies, Chinese cliffs, (these were taken over from the Persian miniature and became more massive in Mughal painting), and by expanses of foliage and the crowns of trees (see Plate 2). The Mughal painters formed thus as many as eight to ten different spaces in the same picture. A zig-zag

29

course of these spaces from the upper to the lower edge of the painting helped to create the illusion of receding space (Plate 3).

In the 17th century the mass of cliffs, buildings and trees is replaced in some of the miniatures by groupings of minor characters, arranged in the form of a wreath, and emphasizing the space set apart for the central figure (see Plate 41 and numerous durbar scenes).

The Mughal method of reproducing volume and mass is also similar to that used in the Ajanta cave-paintings. In both cases a thin shading along the outline is used (Plates 38 and 39). In some Mughal paintings this shading goes deeper, probably as a result of European influence (Ill. IV). Colour contrasts are frequently used to give relief to the mass, especially in the case of the head, pushed into relief by the darker line of the background (Plates 13, 15, 43, 45).

A further deformation of reality is the reduction of the size of the subject to the size of the picture. The Mughal miniature is always a folio, whereas the medieval illustrations were either in the form of a horizontal oblong or of a square cut from a palm leaf. The Islamic miniature tried to create the illusion of a reality continuing beyond the picture by breaking through the margin in several places and allowing parts of buildings or the landscape to overflow from the image. The same device was sometimes also used by the early Rajput painters. The Mughal painters, on the other hand, always kept strictly within the bounds of the picture. If they wished to suggest the continuation of the scene beyond it, they would sometimes cut their figures by the margin, or half-hide them behind the edge of a rock, a building and so on (Plates 2, 4, 6, 26, 34, etc.).

30

Another rather more complicated artistic distortion arises from the need somehow to translate into terms of paint the infinite number and complexity of relationships in time and space. Literature attempts to reconstruct these relationships by breaking up the scene into small units, themes, chapters, scenes and the like in order to reduce it to manageable proportions. Painting, too, resorts to a breakdown of scenes into smaller, self-contained units, groups or pairs of figures. In the Ajanta paintings the groups of figures are held together by the 'receptacles', and the contact between the figures was emphasized by the overcrowding of these restricted spaces. A similar overcrowding may be found in the *Hamza-nama*, where cliffs and trees, even, are crammed together, pinnacle against pinnacle, leaf against leaf. In contrast to all this, the Persian miniature allows each detail of the composition plenty of room, and approaches the problem of their relationship with the same nonchalance as it does that of the third dimension. All the single figures stand apart, and where some kind of relation between figures exists, as where two or three are grouped together, these groups, too, are splendidly isolated (Plate I). The Mughal miniature, on the other hand, evolved in the direction of a harmonious balance between all the elements in the composition. The relationship between each detail extends beyond the confines of the 'receptacles'. The figures are all connected in a loose but dynamic relationship through gesture, facial expression and the adjustment of proportions (Plates 7, 24, 46, 47. Ill. II).

A similar harmony is to be found on a purely formal level in the relation of the individual structural components (heads, limbs, eyes, leaves etc.). The painting of the West Indian illustrations 'exploded' figures and objects into these

31

self-contained formal elements, thus imparting a characteristic rhythm to the composition of the picture. European
and Persian painting, on the other hand, tried to push these
self-contained elements into the background and to present
each object as an organic whole. The Mughal miniature,
particularly in the first half of the 17th century, tended
towards this second conception. The emphasis on partial
forms never quite vanished, however, and the principle of
maximum visibility was applied to them as it was to the
figures (Plates 14, 42, 48). Thus, to take an example, the
individual parts of the body were depicted from different
angles — legs and body in profile, the face in semi-profile
(sometimes in reverse profile as well) (Plate 27). Even
the different parts of the face were quite often portrayed
from different angles. Though the unity of the subject figure
is never quite dissolved — as happens in the West Indian and
some of the Rajput paintings — it never becomes as complete
as it does in European painting, not even in the Mughal
artists' own copies of it (Plate 33).

The development of the miniature, of course, brought
about changes in the stylizations of individual features and
forms — such as the nose, the eye and the scarf. A knowledge
of these changes is very useful in determining questions of
period, individual style and so on. However, it is worth noting
that each of these stylizations developed in conformity with
the general rules governing the art, and that no painter ever
ignored them completely.

This, *mutatis mutandis*, is equally true of the composition, the
distribution of the pictorial area, and, finally, of the basic
constituents of the picture's expressive element, colour and
touch. The colours that originated in the Akbar ateliers,

32

became modified with the passage of time, but their application, either in the delineation of the components, or as part of the rhythmic structure of the painting, remained governed by the principles applicable to Mughal art as a whole.

To give an example, the Mughal painters never use colour in such a way as to reduce the picture to a mere coloured tapestry or mosaic, as do the Persian painters; nor do they beat out the robust rhythm of large coloured areas, so characteristic of some of the local Indian schools. As for brush strokes they depend even more than colour on the personality of the painter; the quality of the line drawing changes, therefore, perceptibly in successive periods of the miniature. Nevertheless, the whole character of Mughal art by its own importance forces the painter to suppress his handwriting and individuality of touch. For this reason, the elegant calligraphic style of the Persian miniature, and the expressive robustness of line of the Rajasthani school, is but seldom found in Mughal art.

All these rules of artistic deformation and stylization, and perhaps even some others, form the main distinctive characteristics of the Mughal miniature. They are its 'grammar'. They have their own logic which governs both the miniatures' development and their relation to other miniatures. It is this unique logic that makes the Mughal miniature a separate and distinct school of painting.

THE GENRES AND PERIODS

No art-form is monomorphic. It appears in different shapes in different social strata, geographical centres and generations of artists, it is differentiated by its function, its genres, etc. For this reason, very few generalisations about art hold good over its entire field. The Mughal miniature is no exception to this rule. For a true understanding of its nature as a whole, we must look at its constituents in more detail.

The question of social milieu creates little difficulty. Mughal painting is court painting pure and simple. In the few cases where a painting left the immediate environs of the court it never penetrated to the commoner. Even those painters who are said to have left the court during the 18th century to establish themselves in the bazaars probably ceased to produce Mughal miniatures in the proper meaning of the word as soon as they were outside the court circle.

A similar situation exists with regard to geographical distribution. Mughal art was tied to the court and moved with it between Fathpur Sikri, Agra and Delhi. Insofar as some workshops existed in the capitals of the Mughal provinces, the work produced in them reflected the political relations of these provinces to the central power. It was closely dependent on the examples produced in the central *ateliers* of the 17th century. In the 18th century, when the provinces became independent states — the *ateliers* in Hyderabad, Murshidabad, Lucknow and other cities became independent too — in fact, the Mughal miniatures had lost their artistic centre. Of these *ateliers* the most important was that of Oudh. It was here that the last revival of the miniature took place, finally to die out in the latter part of the 18th century.

From the aspect of function, the Mughal miniature falls into two sharply-defined groups — the first, the manuscript illustrations, the second, albums and individual

35

paintings. The former was the first to develop. Its main purpose was narrative. It reached its peak under Akbar, and, thereafter, began to decline. The illustrations from the period of Jahangir and his successors are lifeless by comparison with what had gone before.[4]

All subsequent genres derive from the illustrations to Akbar's manuscripts. We see the first signs of breakaway round about 1600 with the formation of the genres that were to lead an independent existence in the albums of Jahangir's and Shah Jahan's eras.

The most celebrated of these genres is the portrait.[5] The fact that, during the 17th century, the Mughal portrait achieved world-wide fame is due to the pioneer work of Basawan and others in the Akbar illustrations. Portraiture was the longest-lived of all the genres, even though by the middle of the 17th century it had lost something of its penetration. The paintings of durbar scenes, celebrating a successful hunting expedition or some similar event, are really mass portraits, and their debt to the manuscript illustrations is even more apparent than that of the individual portraits.

After the portrait, the most famous genre is that of animal and bird painting.[6] The origins of this, too, are to be found in the Akbar illustrations, either of fables or other works.[7] It is doubtful whether Mansur and Manohar would have attained such distinction as animal painters if they had not been able to take over where Miskina left off.

It is rather surprising that landscape painting did not develop into an independent genre, although several starts were made in this direction (in paintings, for instance, such as The Chenar Tree, now in the India Office Library). Jahangir mentions that he had the walls of one of his palaces

36

decorated with paintings of some of the most striking views seen during his summer journey to Kashmir. Unfortunately, he does not seem to have been able to persuade his miniaturists to develop the genre.

Genre painting as such, the portrayal of scenes of everyday life, was also slow to develop. Once again, its roots are to be found in the Akbar illustrations, chiefly in the marginal episodes and in the *zenana* (harem) scenes (Plate 6). This type of painting is seen at its best in the scenes from the lives of sages and hermits, culminating under Shah Jahan in a few pictures that breathe forth the clear atmosphere of the Indian countryside (for instance, the magnificent Tambura Player of Bichitr in the Victoria and Albert Museum). During the 18th century, however, the Indian village appears in numerous genres in an idealized and rococo-styled form.

A third type of painting different in purpose from the illustrations and individual paintings is the illuminated margin (*hashiya*). It makes its first appearance, in imitation of the Persian practice, in some of the first pages of the Akbar manuscripts (*Akbar-nama*, Nizami's *Khamsa*, Jami's *Baharistan*). In the paintings in the albums the traditional arrangement was maintained, whereby the edges of the picture were surrounded by two narrow decorative bands — the first consisting usually of stylized flowers and tendrils — and, secondly, by a broad gilt border in which individual figures and scenes were superimposed upon a conventional floral or landscape background. The Jahangir album, already mentioned, contains the most magnificent of these borders (Plate 9 and some others). Since the borders were purely decorative in purpose (and, thus, considered to be of minor importance) the artist was allowed much more freedom to express himself

37

than in the miniature itself. The fairy-like character of the illumination released him from the demands of naturalism and, at the same time, provided him with a wider range of subjects. As a result, some of the figures and groups are rare examples of artistic freedom and were obviously painted with pleasure and satisfaction. From a few tiny inscriptions we know that some of the most famous painters sometimes worked on these margins (see Govardhan's self-portrait in the margin of one of the folios in the Berlin State Library).[8] In Shah Jahan's time, however, the figures became too big and richly coloured, and lost their animation as a result.

As to the classification of the Mughal miniature according to period the accepted method is according to the reigns of the individual Emperors. It is true that many painters worked under two or more Emperors (Manohar, for instance) and in some cases developed a personal style, but none of them can be said to have formed a school, and their style rarely went outside the limits laid down by the Imperial patron.

For these reasons, we speak of the Akbar *ateliers*, for instance, in the sense of a school or period of art. The *ateliers* were rather like an art-factory. If we find fifty or more names in one manuscript, then the *ateliers* must have employed hundreds of artists at the same time. Together with the foreign-born artists (Abdus Samad, Mir Sayyid Ali and Farrukh Beg) Daswanth and a pleiad of minor stars — Lal, Mukund, Miskina, Keshu, Jagan Nath, Khemkaran and others — emerged as the leading personalities of the Akbar *ateliers*.

After Akbar's death, however, dozens of well-known names never re-appear in the miniatures. This may be because Jahangir's *ateliers* were organized on a different pattern. At the beginning of the reign, Aka Riza (employed by

38

Jahangir before his accession) and his son, Abul Hasan, whom we know as the painter of several durbar scenes, portraits and other works, were probably the leading figures. As time went on, however, they were overshadowed by other artists of Indian origin, portraitists and animal painters. Some of them came from Akbar's *ateliers* (Manohar, Dharanj, Govardhan, Bishndas, Ustad Mansur, Nanha), others were of a new generation (Bichitr, Hashim).

At the beginning of the next reign, that of Shah Jahan, the changes in the *ateliers* were not so far-reaching. Bichitr, an excellent portraitist and genre painter, became the leading personality, and good work was produced by Fateh Chand, Anupchatar and Chitarman. Mir Muhammad Hashim and Muhammad Nadir Samarkandi specialised in portraits of heads in Chinese ink. Towards the end of the reign we come across a certain Hunhar, who worked as a portraitist. He, together, with two other painters succeeded in maintaining his position in Aurangzib's *ateliers*.

In the 18th century (in fact, even under Aurangzib's rule), it becomes increasingly difficult to speak of the Imperial *ateliers* in the previous sense of the term. The classification by reigns also ceases to have much meaning. Only in the case of the eclectic, Mir Khalan Khan, who worked in Lucknow during the second half of the century, does the use of the term 'school' perhaps have some justification.

THE TECHNIQUE

In the history of every art, we find that the materials in which the artist works, play a part in shaping its development. Attempts to make the best use of the material, on the one hand, and the struggle to overcome its limitations, on the other, lead to the discovery of fresh possibilities in the selected medium.

In the case of the Mughal miniature, one of the factors that contributed to its rise was the introduction of paper. Paper had been introduced to India from Persia as early as the beginning of the 15th century. Most of the Jaina manuscripts up to the middle of the 16th century, however, were executed on palm leaves or canvas. Under Akbar, paper was used for the first time to any large extent, but some illustrations and the big corpus of the *Hamza-nama*, are still on canvas. Besides the paper imported from Persia, the Mughal miniaturists also used paper of native manufacture, which was classified according to the material of which it was made (e. g. bamboo paper, jute paper, linen paper, silk paper, etc.). Considerable care was used in the selection of the right type. Once the selection had been made, the chosen sheets were glued together, and the surface of the top one, on which the painting was to be executed, was smoothed and polished with agate.

Next, the outlines were sketched on the prepared surface by means of Indian red without glue. The corrections were carried out in black. Then, the whole drawing was covered with a layer of white and colours were applied to the outlined areas. Finally, the outlines were re-drawn in red, or in a darker shade of the colour in which the figure was painted. The paints were prepared from some twenty-five different

40

pigments, some mineral, some organic. Gum arabic, sugar or linseed oil were used as binding agents.

However, this process, as described, would result merely in a sort of coloured drawing. Had the Mughal painters confined themselves to it they would never have achieved more than the Persian or Rajput painters — an elegance of line and brilliance of colouring. But, in addition, the Mughals used shading to suggest volume. In their portraits, they reached the stage of suppressing the line (without resorting to wash) and of bringing the head into relief by treatment of the background.

These advances were a result of the re-organization of the method of work in the Akbar *ateliers*. Here, the sketch and the 'portrait' would both be executed by one master painter, and the 'execution' left to a lesser-known artist. It would appear from this that most importance was attached to the sketch — the outlining of the basic elements of the composition, the drawing of the outlines and the movement of the figures, etc. — and to the final stage, which was not merely a re-drawing of the outlines, as in the Rajput miniature, but included also a final check on all details of drawing and colouring. The 'execution' consisted of a rough execution of the marked-out composition and a painting-in of the pre-drawn outlines. It is possible that the second artist did not carry out the 'execution' on the original draft, but used it, in fact, as a model for his own work, which was then corrected and finished by the master painter in accordance with his sketch. In several miniatures, both sketch and finished painting have survived. In some cases, several paintings were made from the same sketch. Tracings were also made of the sketches, and stored in the painters' shops, to be used whenever a fresh copy was required. The outlines of the figures in these tracings were perforated, and they were used in the manner of a stencil.

This type of specialisation of work in the Akbar *ateliers*, resulted in an advance from mere coloured line drawings. But, on the other hand, it probably also accounts for a certain lack of rhythm in the composition. Because of this organisation of work the Mughal miniature does not come off so well in comparison with the lively rhythm of line of the Persian schools and the rhythm of the coloured masses of Rajput art.

THE OTHER SCHOOLS

Some thirty years ago, Stchoukine aptly observed that the phenomenon of hybridization in art, so frequent in the Mughal and other neo-Indian schools, provides the art-historian with valuable evidence of how different styles come into being. He pointed out that the Mughal miniature may appear as an imitation of Persian painting or as an indigenous affair according to whether we look at it from the point of view of Persian art or Indian art. He himself believed that the 'centre towards which all disparate elements gravitate' was to be found in the Indian tradition. What precisely he meant by this tradition, however, he did not make clear.

The tendency of scholars today is to accept Mughal painting on its own terms, to view it from its own standpoint, as a completely independent form. Indian scholars of the group round Khandalawala go further and see the Mughal school as the centre of other schools of Indian miniature painting. Rai Krishnadasa states bluntly that 'the Mughal school of painting formed, as it were, the spinal column of the various

43

schools of Indian miniature art. If the Mughal school had not come into being, the Pahari and Rajasthani schools would not have emerged in the forms in which we find them'. The autonomous position of the Mughal school may be deduced from the fact that it evolved its own aesthetic canon, and that any painting departing from it and showing pronounced Persian, Indian or European influence may, according to Skelton, 'immediately be seen in relief and its distance from the main stream may in some measure be assessed'.

Once we accept the autonomy of the Mughal miniature then the question of its relationship with other schools becomes a question of the degree to which the elements of other styles are present in its make-up or have become absorbed into it.

Let us look at the question of the relationship between the Mughal miniature and Buddhist mural painting, the first Indian manifestation of the art. A thousand years, at least, separate the two, and scholars trying to establish a native ancestry of any standing for the miniatures usually run into difficulties. The Tibetan monk, Taranatha, in his *History of Indian Buddhism*, published in 1608, hints at a continuation of Ajanta art into succeeding centuries, but it is hard to determine from his account where history ends and legend begins. He mentions a division of the Buddhist tradition along geographical lines into an 'ancient Western school' and an 'Eastern school', referring to the central Indian branch of the latter as the 'Magadha style', and traces the emergence of minor local schools in Kashmir, southern India and elsewhere. Goetz devoted considerable effort to tracing the historical source of Taranatha's information,[9] and found a continuation of the 'Eastern school' in the Nepalese manuscripts of the 11th and 12th centuries. He concluded that the

44

characteristic features of this school were introduced into the Mughal miniature by Gwalior painters (for instance, the 'lancet' as compared with the Western 'almond' type of eye). Some elements of the 'Western school' may have survived in Gujarat and Rajasthan, and may, perhaps, be seen in the Kashmir paintings published by Professor Tucci.

Although it may not be possible to prove the historical connection between ancient Buddhist art and that of the Mughal miniature, it seems highly probable, nonetheless, that such a connection existed. The painters swarming into Akbar's *ateliers* came from all parts of India — Kashmir, Lahore, Gujarat, Gwalior, Rajasthan and so on. The earliest illustrations in the *Hamza-nama* show many traces of the influence of the Buddhist tradition, and this influence played a very distinct part in the final formulation of the Mughal style. Buddhist elements may be discerned in the modelling of the eye, in the 'Ajantan' softness of the arms, and in the use of the so-called 'multiple perspective' in the interpretation of space. This method is to be found nowhere else.

Certain elements of the 'ancient Western school' probably also survived in the medieval illustrated manuscripts of the Jain school. This is also known as the Gujarat or Western Indian school and flourished from the 12th to 16th century.

Its main characteristics are an extreme stylization, flatness, hierarchical perspective and an emphasized delineation of the self-contained components (e. g. heads, limbs, leaves, eyes etc.) by means of colour and line. The relationship of Mughal art to this painting is analogous to the relationship of the Urdu language to the older Apabhramsha languages — and, perhaps, more dynamic. For Mughal art strove from the beginning to emancipate itself from the medieval tradition, and to replace

45

it in all its aspects with innovations borrowed from wherever they were available. Its endeavours were successful, but something of the medieval tradition always remained. The stress laid on the self-contained components never quite disappeared, although in their copying of Persian and European works the Mughal painters must have followed the trend towards presenting the object as an uninterrupted unity.

The Rajasthani miniature is a sister of the Mughal miniature, as Hindi is a sister of Urdu. It, too, felt the need to break away from the influence of the medieval manuscript painting, but as it was less quick to absorb non-Indian elements, its struggle was fiercer, longer and more dramatic. The question of its relationship with the Mughal school has often been discussed,[10] but no agreement has ever been reached as to which is the older. During the formative period in the 16th century the Mughal and Rajput conceptions were in a balanced partnership. The so-called Rajput elements are as frequent a feature in the paintings from Akbar's *ateliers* as the Mughal elements in the early Rajput miniatures. In fact, in some cases it is highly controversial whether a painting is to be classified as Mughal or Rajput. It was ascertained, however, that after 1600 A. D. the Mughal miniature was associated with the central power, whereas Rajasthan painting was an expression of the feudal Rajput organisation. Where they looked similar in form, they were different in content. The Rajasthan painting may have had more vitality, but the Mughal miniature was more powerful. When Mughal art began to lose ground in the second part of the 17th century, Rajput art was quick to seize the advantage, and in the following century Rajput concepts came to occupy a dominating position in Mughal art, which in the end, melted into

46

the local Rajput schools in the same way as the central power of the Mughal Empire melted into the provinces.

Another related miniature is that of the Deccan. We are still not sure, however, of the exact degree of its relationship with the Mughal school. Many so-called Deccanese stylistic details have been enumerated (their number keeps on increasing) yet no attribution of a miniature to the school is ever quite free of doubt. Such, for example, is the case of the miniature in Plate 8. We should not hesitate to take it for a Deccanese painting, were it not for the fact that a Mughal court painter is mentioned as its author. The exact position of Deccanese painting will probably soon be established. Meanwhile, it is interesting to note that at the beginning it resembled Mughal art very closely.

It appeared round about the same time and incorporated both Persian and native elements, particularly those of the Vijayanagara tradition. Later on, the Indian features prevailed and since this art was the product of the feudal organisation in the southern Indian states, it came nearer in style to the Rajasthani miniature.

The problem of the relation between Mughal and Persian painting is a difficult one. The Persian influence tends to be either over- or underestimated, and it seems impossible to hit upon an exact mean. There may be a reason for this: the Mughal and the Persian miniatures are not strictly comparable and thus the question is not a proper one. The Mughal miniature is a uniform structure, the product of one country and one period of history; the so-called Persian miniature, on the other hand, is a complex of different schools and styles. It is the product of the cosmopolitan culture of Islam, which had no definite centre; it flared up from time to time in many

47

places — in Shiraz, Herat, Samarkand, Bukhara, and last but not least, in Agra, Fathpur Sikri and Delhi under the Mughals. The standard-bearers of this culture came and went, and only their surnames and accents provide a clue to their birthplace and the masters who taught them. Such is the case with the Persian and Central Asian painters who reached the Mughal court. Goetz has remarked that these painters introduced to Mughal painting the style of two centres, but if we wanted we could find many more such centres. How unimportant this question really is may be seen from the career of Farrukh Beg (Plate 8).

In 1585, when Farrukh came to Akbar's *ateliers* from Shiraz by way of Khorasan and Kabul, he brought with him a Central Asian accent that earned him the designation of 'Beg'. No sooner had Akbar begun to suppress Islamic cosmopolitanism in favour of the native Indian culture, than Farrukh felt it advisable to look for a new master, and left for the Deccan (where he certainly taught the younger painters the Mughal style). When the cosmopolitan Islamic style began to show signs of returning to favour under young Jahangir, Farrukh returned to the Mughal court — this time as a painter in the Deccanese manner. If he had been rather younger than his seventy years, he would probably, when Jahangir reversed his policy round about 1615, have set out once more on his travels and been certain of a welcome anywhere — this time as a painter in the Mughal (i. e. Jahangir) style.

As to the relation of the Mughal miniature to other Islamic paintings it is probably true to say that Islamic painting contained elements alien to the Indian native tradition, which never became a lasting constituent of Mughal art, and that Mughal painting is distinguished by several char-

48

acteristics that cannot be found in other forms of Islamic painting. The elements which never became fully incorporated in Mughal painting appear in two or three waves, only to disappear again, or to become modified.

Among these elements are the consistent two-dimensionality of Persian painting, the perspective that combines a bird's-eye view of landscape with a direct view of the figures (Plate 21); the restricting of movement to stereotyped gestures, and of natural features — trees, cliffs and the like — to a few types (Plate 23); the complete isolation of figures and pairs of figures, and the absence of confrontation between most of them (Plate 1); the reproduction of intricate patterns in carpets and the elevations of buildings; and the arbitrary distortion of the palette, so that the picture takes on the appearance of a coloured tapestry. Finally, there is the over-calligraphic line that derives from the predominantly literary character of Islamic culture. All these features are outside the normal canon of Mughal painting and never become a permanent part of it.

European painting first appeared within the horizon of the Islamic miniaturist in Turkey at the turn of the 15th century. But it was in India, at the Mughal court, that it received the warmest welcome. Akbar did not allow any feeling of respect for Moslem orthodoxy to influence his patronage, and he welcomed Indian and European painting impartially. Jesuit missionaries from Goa, in 1580 and later, expounded the European aesthetic to him. He passed on to the painters in his *ateliers* examples of European religious painting, illustrations from Plantin's eight-volume Bible and other European engravings, recommending that they should study them and profit by them. In 1588, Keshava Das presented the Emperor with an album of copies that he had made of European religious paintings, while Basawan, of a more creative nature, gave up copying in order to apply European principles to his own work (Plate 6).

Jahangir was quite capable of delivering an informed judgement on European works. Fernao Guerreiro, William Finche, and Hawkins, who all visited his court round about 1610, report, with a fair degree of unanimity, that parts of Jahangir's palace were adorned with European pictures. Manucci in his study, *Storia di Magor*, says that he himself saw the Christian pictures with which Jahangir had decorated Akbar's tomb in Sikandra, and which, later on, were destroyed by order of Aurangzib. The most reliable contemporary evidence is probably that of Sir Thomas Roe, Ambassador to the Mughal court from 1616 to 1618. In his reports to the East India Company he warns that the Emperor was quite capable of distinguishing between good and bad, and that they should be careful not to send him any second-rate pictures. He records carefully the pictures that met with the Emperor's approval and the way in which they were received.

From Father Guerreiro's account, it appears that European painting was also appreciated by many outside the circle of the court, and that a large copy of the Roman Madonna, *S. Maria del Popolo*, which arrived in Agra in 1602, aroused the admiration of the crowds. It seems, indeed, that the Mughal painters found no difficulty in understanding European painting, and that they were, in fact, influenced by it, particularly in the expression of depth and volume. Wilkinson ascribes this to the tradition among Indian artists of viewing objects in the round.

The whole of Asian painting between the 16th and 18th

50

centuries, at some time or other, shows the results of contact with European painting, although in many different ways. But the European style almost certainly attained its greatest influence in the Mughal miniature, where some of its techniques were completely absorbed. European pictures were most often and most straightforwardly copied at the Mughal court.

However, the principles of European painting penetrated to the core of Mughal art only insofar as it was in conformity with the intrinsic evolution of this art. The European convergent perspective, for example, was often used in a wide range of landscape backgrounds, but its application was never wholly consistent, as it was never drawn from a single focal point. The European type of shading was used to convey the impression of volume, but only in certain types of object, and never to produce the effect of *chiaroscuro*. It is interesting to note, also, that the Mughal sovereigns never attempted to introduce into their *ateliers* European oil-painting and graphic technique, which they very obviously held in contempt. According to Roe, Jahangir refused to accept two paintings, which being 'in oyle, he liked it not'.

Another style of painting with which the Mughal miniature had some point of contact was that of China. This reached the Mughal school primarily as part of Islamic painting which it had penetrated *via* Central Asia (Plate 19). It is not impossible, however, that Chinese influence may have affected the Mughal court directly, since chinaware and other products of the minor arts were imported through Bijapur (as we know from Roe's notes). According to one source, the walls of one palace in Fathpur Sikri were decorated with Chinese plum-flowers and the conventional clouds. In one miniature, taken from the same manuscript as the folio in Plate 1, shrubs and

51

birds appear which are strongly reminiscent of those in Chinese pictures. But such evidence, of course, is hardly enough to support any theory of fresh impulses coming into Mughal painting directly from Chinese art.

A similar problem that defies solution is that of the connection between the Mughal miniature and the mural paintings to be found in some of the architecture of the period. Literature, it is true, is full of accounts of the way in which the walls of Akbar's and Jahangir's buildings were decorated, but none of these paintings has survived. Such knowledge as we have of these mural paintings has come to us through their appearance in the miniatures; these show that the plant motifs of Akbar's day were less conventional in design than those of the famous murals of Shah Jehan's time. It is difficult to imagine what the figural motifs were like. The painters of the murals were probably not the same as those of the miniatures, yet literature contains no reference to two staffs of painters.

THE ENVIRONMENT

Much time and effort has been spent by scholars in trying to determine the relatively unimportant question of the national character of Mughal art. Is it, for example, more Indian than Persian? Or more Irano-Indian than Europeo-Indian? Is it the flowering of Moslem culture in India, or the Indianisation of Islamic art?

The Mughal miniature is, quite simply, a Mughal art. It is a component part of reality, and that reality is that of the Mughal era.

54

Some knowledge therefore of Mughal life is essential if we are to see Mughal art in correct perspective. Let us select three aspects of this life and examine them in relation to the Mughal miniature: first, the society to which this art appealed, its political and economic conditions; second, the originators (artists and patrons) who expressed themselves through the art; and thirdly the cultural environment which was depicted, reflected and explained by the art.

Looking at the political and economic background, we find that, as Goetz has pointed out, the rise of Mughal painting was closely connected with the transition of the country from the medieval to the modern era. This 'modern' era, however, was only potentially present in Mughal India; it never developed in the same way as it did in Europe. The preceding period of Afghan domination has been described by Pandit Nehru as a backward feudal and tribal order; the Mughal Empire, in contrast, may be thought of as a semi-feudal order with a strong monarchical centre. This centre consisted of the Emperor himself and his military bureaucracy — that is to say an aristocracy, weakened by the loss of its medieval sources of strength, the ownership of land and hereditary title, but still endowed with considerable power and privilege. It was a very heterogeneous body: Turks, Afghans and Persians ranked equally with Indian Rajputs, Moslems with Hindus.

It is generally agreed that his alliance with the Rajput ruling class was the shrewdest political move of the third Mughal Emperor, Akbar. As a result, he not only strengthened the government, the army and the bureaucracy, but brought into existence a national State. This first demolition of religious, racial and cultural barriers marked an important stage in

55

the transition of India from medieval to modern times. Jahangir, it is true, at the beginning of the following century showed a disposition towards Moslem orthodoxy, but he soon returned to the political conception of his father. It was only in the second part of the century that the trend towards a unified national State was reversed by Aurangzib, and it led the Empire towards inevitable disaster.

Mughal art was extremely sensitive to these political developments. They were reflected both in changes in its style and in its recording of the changes taking place in society. The building of the national State and the welding together of the indigenous and foreign elements are reflected in the illustrations from the last decades of the 16th century. Jahangir's change of policy for some years almost deprived the miniature of its newly-won autonomy (Plates 10, 22, 23). Under Aurangzib, whose rule more closely resembled that of a Turkish Sultan than that of an Indian Emperor, the Mughal miniature falls from its previous heights as though it had been struck by an arrow.

This contrast between the tremendous vitality of the art at its inception, and the impotence that overtook it after its early successes is startling. In all probability it is a result of the conflict between the revolutionary and progressive changes of the Mughal era and their inconsistencies and imperfections.

Akbar built up a brilliantly successful structure of government, as a result of which the Crown ceased to be dependent on its vassals. This centralisation, however, did not reach the villages which retained their medieval autonomy. Raja Todar Mall, an economist of genius, introduced a reform of the tax system which strengthened not only the Imperial Treasury but also the economic condition of the whole Empire. Yet, by the middle of the 17th century the new tax system had begun to degenerate into the old lease system. Akbar built up an immense power on land, but he was defenceless at sea; he failed to grasp the growing importance of naval power in deciding the fate of the world. He recruited and organised a splendid army, the core of which was cavalry, yet he neglected artillery, which was left to Turkish instructors and cannons. He was enormously inquisitive, as we know from the contemporary accounts of missionaries; everything interested him, anything new captured his attention. He knew of the discovery of America, he familiarised himself with the techniques of European printing, he wanted clocks to be imported, and so on. But he took no steps to introduce these mechanical advances into his own realms and to establish a native industry in these particular products.

Contemporary European and Indian writers describe the enormous wealth, prosperity and general well-being of the Empire under Akbar, and, in particular, the cheapness of food. But neither Akbar nor his successors were able to prevent dreadful famines in 1573 and again from 1630 to 1632. The industrial activity was, according to modern historians, one of the outstanding features of Mughal India. In the mid-17th century, India led the world in the production of cotton and silk, in dye-works, and in the output of indigo and saltpetre. Yet, in the last decade of the century, English ships were unable to find enough cargo to fill their holds. Contrasts such as these show the strength and weakness of the Mughal Empire; they were strikingly reflected in the development of the Mughal miniature. Naturally, this development remained unaffected by such trifles as the establishment of English, Portuguese and Dutch factories and trading posts. But it was these outposts, almost unnoticed by the rulers of India, that came to dominate the history of the country during the eighteenth century and led, finally, to the establishment of British rule over the sub-continent. With this new order of things the Mughal miniature had no links and passed from the stage for ever.

The second factor that played a part of some importance in the evolution of the miniature was the position of the artists and their patrons. Europeans are often tempted to make an absolute identification between the artist and his work. But, in fact, even during periods of the most exaggerated individualism, the artist is never completely comprised in his work, and the expressive function of art has never been the only one. This is the more true outside Europe.

In Indian art the position of the patron has always been important. The relationship between artist and patron and the changes in their attitude towards art are distinctive features in the history of Indian painting. If we look at the period immediately preceding the Mughal miniature, we shall see that the miniature introduced a great change in this respect. In the Jainist illustrations of the 15th century neither the artist nor his patron (the Gujarati merchant) revealed his individuality, and the setting and composition of the paintings were always subordinated to the prevailing convention. The position did not change throughout the first three-quarters of the following century. As long as he worked at the royal court or at that of a nobleman the artist was not paid. He received, instead, an allowance of provisions, hereditary in his family, regardless of what he did or how.

The first two Mughal Emperors, as we have already mentioned, took a personal interest in painting. They had

58

their own ideas on the subject, and one of these, that they had been taught at the Persian court, was that the artist of genius may and has to express himself in his work to a certain degree.

It was very probably Akbar who revolutionised the tradition by erecting spacious *ateliers* for his artists and constantly checking their achievement. His biographer tells us that 'His Majesty has since his youth exhibited a predilection for the art of painting, which he supported in all possible ways, for he thought it both a means to knowledge and pleasure at the same time. Art, therefore, prospered and many painters attained great honours'. Akbar is said to have visited his *ateliers* every week and given special rewards to the most successful painters. He gave orders for certain books to be illustrated, sat for his portrait, took painters with him on his military expeditions, made them officers, even entrusted them with the command of armies. He told his courtiers to follow his example, ordered them to engage painters, to commission copies of illustrated manuscripts, and to have their portraits painted. He probably had to overcome stubborn resistance on this latter point from the orthodox Moslems. 'Bigoted interpreters of the scriptures bear a grudge against painting,' reports Abul Fazl. This faithful friend of the Emperor seems, himself, to have gone through a considerable internal struggle, for we find him saying: 'I must say that the act of contemplating figures and objects and of their portrayal, frequently considered as a work in vain, is for a spirit endowed with a source of knowledge an antidote against the poison of ignorance.' Among Akbar's courtiers, the highly cultivated Abdur Rahim Khan-i-Khanan (at one time, Commander-in-Chief of the armies) became a patron of painting, and we know that he

59

employed several painters, as did Prince Salim, the later
Emperor Jahangir.

The Emperor's direct interest and initiative were probably
among the determining factors in the development of the
Mughal miniature during the third quarter of the 16th century.
The majority of the painters although 'they attained great
honours' probably remained in the background. Important
positions, no doubt, were held by the two Persian masters,
Mir Sayyid Ali and Abdus Samad (the second of whom later
became Manager of the Imperial Mint in Delhi), and, among
the Indian painters, by Daswanth, the madman of genius who
later committed suicide, and by Basawan. Akbar's chronicle
has more to say about their art. A further thirteen painters
are mentioned by name, and then it goes on: 'Over a hundred
painters became famous masters of their art and the number
of those who attained perfection or were of the middle rank
is considerable.' All these painters, all of whom were members
of the lower castes and hardly ever rose above the status of
artisans, contributed to the formation of the Mughal style,
although they 'did not reveal distinct individual traits'
(Wilkinson).[11]

A feature peculiar to the Akbar *ateliers* was collective work.
On certain sheets in some of the manuscripts we may come
across the notes of scribes, from which it is evident that the
sketch, the execution, and the detail of the portraits are the
work of two or three different painters. To their names the
words *tarkh* (work), *am'l* (execution) and *chihra-numa* (portrait)
are appended. Stchoukine attributes 'this bizarre system' to
the whim of the Emperor or to a tradition imported from
Persia. Others have seen in it a victory for the traditional
Indian system of collective painting. It seems possible, on the

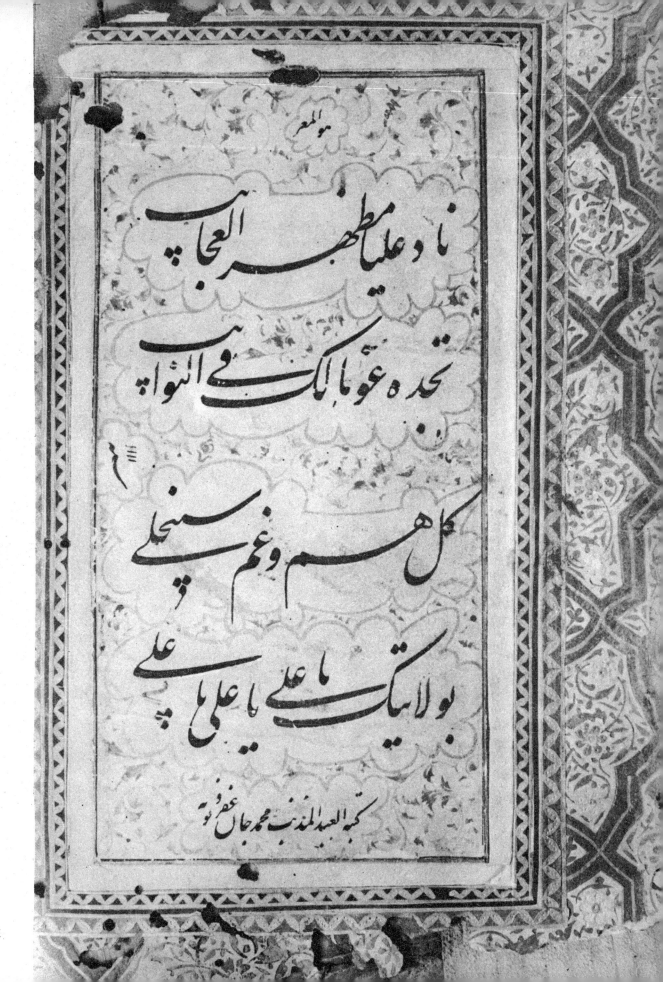

other hand, that techniques being developed in the manufacturing trades at this time may have exerted an influence. The painters' *ateliers* were only one of the numerous workshops attached to the court, in which the factory system of specialisation was developing. We know, among other things, that this specialisation existed in the preparation of the artists' materials — one group prepared the surface of the paper, another the pigments, a third the brushes; it may have seemed logical that the process should be extended to the actual work of painting.

If this assumption is correct, then the conditions that developed under Jahangir are more readily comprehensible. Here, the specialisation originated in the Akbar *ateliers* continued, and we find each painter employing his special talent in the particular genres that appeal to him — Ustad Mansur in animal and bird paintings, Bishndas in group portraiture, Govardhan in official scenes, Farrukh Beg in traditional Persian motifs, Muhammad Nadir in Chinese-ink drawings of heads, and so on. Thus, under Jahangir and Shah Jahan, many painters developed a relatively well-marked personal style. This was the maximum freedom ever attained by the Mughal artist. 'In any picture submitted to me,' writes Jahangir in his memoirs, 'I can guess the name of its creator.'

However, the patron's share in the work remained prominent. Jahangir, in particular, a fanatical collector and lover of paintings, guided the work of his artists to a marked degree. We read in his memoirs how he set the subjects and how carefully supervised their execution. His artists were 'Jahangir made'. He says of the painter, Abul Hasan: 'I watched him from his earliest youth until the moment when he became a painter of such an excellent order as he now is.'

62

In the last years of Jahangir's reign the influence of his highly cultivated and influential wife, Nur Jahan, also became felt in the world of art. We find appearing, in the miniature, tendencies already apparent in the architecture built to her orders. By a similar comparison, the influence of the great builder, the Emperor Shah Jahan, may be descried in the whole trend of the miniatures of his reign. The opinions of his son, Dara Shikoh, also certainly influenced the miniature of the second quarter of the 17th century.

Mention has previously been made of the results flowing from Aurangzib's refusal to patronise painting or the arts generally. During his reign many painters were forced to leave the court and seek refuge with the local aristocracy. Those who remained at the court, worked in the households of courtiers, or of the Princes and Princesses (for instance, that of Aurangzib's daughter, Zeb-un-Nisa). From the patronage of the Emperor they descended to that of the harem, to the status of jugglers, dancers and courtesans. This is reflected in the subject-matter as well as in the quality of their works. In conclusion, we may say that in Mughal painting the expressive function was more pronounced than in any other branch of Indian art. The development of the Mughal miniature was closely connected with the personalities of its patrons, and, to a lesser degree, with the personalities of the artists themselves.

The third major factor relevant to the development of the Mughal miniature was the state of the general culture of the time. Here, the mutual relationship developed along several lines. In general, the relationship between the art of painting and the general culture was similar to that between painting and the social, economic and political environment. One important feature of Mughal culture was the gradual blending

63

of the Islamic and native Hindu elements, and this was reflected in the miniature, as we have already seen.

Of the complex of forms and disciplines that go to make up Mughal culture as a whole, we have already noticed the parallelism between architecture and painting at a certain stage of the development of each. A similar parallelism may be traced in other spheres — in literature, in music, in language (the Mughal miniature develops side by side with the Urdu language), in religion and education.

A connection of a different kind between painting and the general culture may be seen in the fact that the Mughal miniature depicts many different aspects of the day. The changing fashions of dress are of special interest here. (Goetz has made a study of these on the basis of pictorial evidence.) We may also follow the changing fashions in the architecture through the medium of the miniatures. Nevertheless, the Mughal miniature's relations to the individual cultural pheno-mena of the day are not of primary importance. There is no aesthetic or ideological connection between them; they do not help to explain one another. In this respect the Mughal miniature differs from other types of Indian painting (e.g. Rajasthani painting).

CONCLUSION

In conclusion, let me briefly recapitulate the main points of the previous chapters.

First, the Mughal miniature developed its own set of rules governing style, the artistic deformation and stylization of reality. These rules were quite different from those that applied

64

in other branches of Indian or Islamic art. They were never contravened except in paintings on the fringe of the art or in the works of strongly creative individuals. Major alterations in the established rules occurred during transitional periods between one stage of the art's evolution and the next. During the first hundred years or so of Mughal art, these stages corresponded with the reigns of individual Emperors. The basic possibilities of the art arising from the techniques and materials used by the painters, were modified in practice by the collective method of working peculiar to the Mughal *ateliers*.

Secondly, with regard to the relation of the Mughal miniature to other periods and schools of paintings, we find that some of the conventions of the ancient Indian cave-paintings are to be found underlying Mughal art. The medieval illustrations of Western India form a background to older conventions; in the Mughal miniature their place is taken by new features. These innovations were derived partly from the various Persian schools (in two or three successive waves), partly from indigenous contemporary trends and partly from European painting. Other branches of the Indian miniature — the Rajasthani, the Pahari, the Deccani — appear as sister forms; the Mughal style most closely approaches them during the opening and closing stages of its evolution.

Thirdly, in its evolution the Mughal miniature reacted very sensitively to changes in its political and economic environment. Imperial patronage played the decisive role in its development, but sometimes a painter's individual touch can be discerned. As far as social milieu is concerned, the court circle was the miniaturist's only public. There was comparatively little contact with other branches of contemporary art.

Finally, in spite of the non-spontaneous and rather hot-house nature of its development, the Mughal miniature bequeathed to Indian art as a whole values that became an integral part of it, and made no small contribution to the culture of Islam and of the world.

NOTES

[1] See the so-called Jahangir Album, published in 1924 by Kühnel and Goetz.

[2] See Stchoukine, *La peinture indienne à l'époque des grands Moghols*, Paris, 1929. This is a basic analysis of form. The author examines the stylization of Nature, animals and people, and the character of the composition in the Mughal miniature and in some of the related schools.

[3] See Madame S. Kramisch, *A Survey of Paintings in the Deccan*, London, 1937, and Stchoukine, *op. cit.*

[4] See the three manuscripts published by Pinder-Wilson and Wilkinson in *Ars Orientalis, Vol. II*, Washington, 1957, pp. 413–425.

[5] See Coomaraswamy in the *Orientalisches Archiv, Vol. III;* Stchoukine in the *Revue des Arts Asiatiques, Vols. VI, VII & IX;* Eastman in the *Journal of Near Eastern Studies, Vol. XV;* and others.

[6] See Blunt in *The Burlington Magazine*, 1948; Kumar Saraswati in *Marg, Vol. II;* and others.

[7] E. g. the Moscow copy of the *Babur-nama.*

[8] *Eastern Art, II*, Philadelphia, 1930, Plate II.

[9] In 'Die Malschulen des Mittelalters und die Anfänge der Moghul-Malerei', *Ostasiatische Zeitschrift*, 1926, NF III, pp. 173-187 and elsewhere.

[10] See Gray, *Intermingling of Mughal and Rajput Art*. India, Vol. 3, Part. 1, 1954, pp. 59—66.

[11] Staude has devoted a series of exhaustive studies to the identification of idiosyncrasies of style of some of Akbar's most important painters, for instance, Basawan, Daswanth, Miskina and L-ab. (See Illustration II. Plates 4 and 5.)

66

LIST OF COLOUR PLATES AND ILLUSTRATIONS

1. Akbar at his Court. Folio from Nizami's Khamsa illustrated manuscript. Size 16 by 11 cm. Teheran Archaeological Museum. C. 1595 The margin later.

The Teheran Archaeological Museum contains another folio from the same manuscript (erroneously classified as a Persian miniature) showing a group of scholars in front of a building in the Fathpur Sikri style with murals. The stylization of the landscape, as in this miniature, is Indian, although the figures are dressed in Persian garments. Both miniatures are very similar in style to some illustrations in the *Hamza-nama* and in the *Razm-nama*. The central figure in this miniature may be the Emperor Akbar. If so, this is probably an authentic portrait, for a similar likeness appears in the *Akbar-nama* in scenes after 1570.

2. Encounter with a Princess. P. 620 of the illustrated manuscript of Rashid-ud-din's History of the Mongols (Jami-ut-Tawarikh). Teheran Imperial Library. C. 1595.

The calligraphic text in Nastaliq characters is dated 1004 H. (1595—1596 A. D.) Most of the illustrations to this manuscript are the work of Basawan, Miskina and Farrukh. They amount to ninety-eight in all.

3. Crossing of the Ganges by the Armies of Kubla Khan. P. 327 of the same manuscript.

4. Master Rashid-ud-din's Commissioning (with the writing of the History). P. 3 of the same manuscript. Painted by Basawan. Detail of the lower part. The text is glued into the picture.

Basawan was one of the most famous painters of the Akbar *ateliers*. The contemporary chronicler, Abul Fazl, says of him in the annals, *Ain-i-Akbari:* '... he is best in depicting the background, in drawing, in the distribution of colours, in portraiture and in other branches.' An exhaustive study of Basawan's style was published by W. Staude in the *Revue des Arts Asiatiques* (Tome VIII, Paris, 1932, 'Contribution à l'étude de Basawan', pp. 1—18) and in *Arts Asiatiques* (Tome II, Paris, 1955, 'Les artistes de la cour d'Akbar et les illustrations du Dastan-i-Amir Hamzah', pp. 43—65 and 83—111).

5. *Ghazan Khan Armies. P. 514 of the same manuscript. Painted by Miskina. Detail of the upper part.*
The painter, Miskina (or Miskin) is one of the seventeen painters of importance mentioned by name in the chronicle, *Ain-i-Akbari*. His special gift for animal portraiture is noted by Staude. (*Op. cit.* (1955) pp. 86—89).

6. *The Burglars' Escape from the Palace. Loose sheet. Size 215 by 123 mm. Teheran Archaeological Museum. Attributed to Basawan. C. 1595. The margin later.*
If the attribution is correct, this painting is one of Basawan's best works (together with the Scene of a Princess's Reception, in the *Darab-nama* manuscript (British Museum), and the Scene of Sheikh Abul Kessab's Conversation with a Dervish, in the *Baharistan* manuscript (Bodleian)). It approaches them in composition, conception of space, stylization of the drapery, and in the vivacity of the figures. (See Staude, *op. cit.*).

69

7. Women in the Harem. Loose sheet. Size 154 by 125 mm. Teheran Archaeological Museum. Attributed to Farrukh Beg. C. 1610.

There is nothing among the known works of Farrukh Beg comparable in style with this miniature. (See R. Skelton, 'The Mughal artist, Farrokh Beg', *Ars Orientalis*, Vol. II, Washington, 1957, pp. 393—411). The Teheran attribution, therefore, seems very problematical. If we accept it, however, this painting would most probably date from the artist's last period (see below), as the types of faces and the costume suggest the Deccan. The miniature most closely resembles the painting, The Sleeping Maidens (Berlin), classified by Goetz as a Hyderabad work of the early 18th century. ('Indian Miniatures in German Museums and Private Collections', *Eastern Art, Vol. II*, Philadelphia, 1930. p. 169). However, the attribution to the beginning of the 17th century seems the most likely for both these works, regardless of whether they were painted at the Mughal court or in the South.

8. The Bijapuri Shah, Ibrahim Adil Shah II (1580—1629). A folio from Jahangir's Album. Size 420 by 625 mm, including margin. In the upper part, two European engravings; the margin, with golden tendrils of flowers and coloured birds. The inner margin bears the following inscription: 'Portrait of Ibrahim Adil Khan of Deccan, Prince of Bijapur, who through his knowledge of music brought fame to Deccan and enlightenment to his people. He condescended to show favour to Farrukh Beg's work by sitting for him in the year 1019 (A.D. 1610—1611). Written by Muhammad Huseyn Zarin Kalan, the slave of Jahangir.' Náprstek Museum, Prague.

This folio was probably part of the so-called Jahangir and Golshan Album (see below). It is of considerable historical

70

X

importance for two reasons. First, it is a contemporary portrait of the Bijapur ruler, as is borne out by the inscription. Most of the portraits of this sovereign were not executed before the end of the 17th and the beginning of the 18th centuries, and some of these bear no inscriptions at all. (See Moti Chandra, 'Portraits of Ibrahim Adil Shah II', *Marg, Vol. V, No. 1*, Bombay, 1951, pp. 22 ff.; and R. Skelton, 'Documents for the Study of Painting at Bijapur', *Arts Asiatiques, Tome V, Vol. 2*, Paris, 1958, pp. 97—125). So far, the most authentic portrait of the monarch is a miniature recently discovered in the library of the Lallgarh Palace, Bikaner (Colour reproduction, S. Kramisch, *The Art of India*, London, 1955, Plate IV). The name, however, was inscribed later, in 1748. In it, Ibrahim Adil Shah is depicted as approximately the same age as in the present picture, if not a little older. The likeness of the dark courtier (see Plate 12), on the whole, also tallies.

A second peculiarity of this miniature is the fact that it seems to bear out Skelton's theory that Farrukh Beg worked for several years at the Bijapur court, and that he is the same as the painter, Farrukh Huseyn, mentioned in the works on the Bijapur history (See Skelton, *op. cit.* in *Ars Orientalis II*). We may also accept, therefore, Skelton's other deductions about the life of the artist. According to him, Farrukh Huseyn was probably the son of the Shiraz scholar and illuminator, Maulana Darwish. In his early youth, he emigrated to Khorasan, from where, after the death of his local patron, Ibrahim Mirza, in 1576, he went to Kabul and, thence, in 1585, into Akbar's *ateliers* in Agra, where he collaborated in the illustration of some of the manuscripts. In 1601, he was sent as an envoy to Bijapur, where

72

he exercised a very important influence on the local school of painting. He returned to the Mughal court before 1609, for Jahangir mentions in his memoirs that he rewarded him that year with 2,000 rupees. He stayed with Jahangir until about 1615, when he died.

It is not clear whether he painted this portrait (and some other miniatures in the Deccanese style) before or after his return to the Mughal court. On the whole, the former seems the more probable. The figures were probably painted from models. In the chronology of Farrukh Beg's works, compiled by Skelton, this portrait should be placed round about the year 1605.

9. *Mir Ali's Calligraphy and Decorative Margin. Reverse of the following folio.*

The broad margin (*hashiya*) with its golden sprays of flowering plants, and coloured birds on one side, and a fanciful landscape with figures on the other, adorned all the folios of Jahangir's personal album. This, without any doubt, was the finest achievement of Mughal art during the 17th century. Up till now some 120 folios have been discovered. The bulk of the album, some 88 folios, in the Teheran Archaeological Museum, is known as the Golshan Album. Though it formed part of the Exhibition of Persian Art in London in 1933, only a few of the miniatures were published by Binyon in the Catalogue. (See *Persian Miniature Painting*, London, 1933; and Godard, 'Les Marges du Marakka Golshan', *Annales du Service Archaeologique de l'Iran*, Paris, 1936). A further 8 folios were recently purchased by the Shah's Imperial Library and were lent to Prague in 1956 (some of these miniatures and marginal details are reproduced in Plates 21—32). Another part of the original album was brought to Europe in 1861 by the Prussian Ambassador to Persia. Of this section, 21 folios are kept in the Berlin Library (see E. Kühnel and H. Goetz, *Indische Buchmalerei aus dem Jahangir Album der Staatsbibliothek zu Berlin*, Berne, 1924, supplemented by an enlarged English edition, London, 1926), and several loose sheets are in other European collections (Marteau, Sohn-Rethel). Two folios in the Náprstek Museum in Prague have not hitherto been reproduced and appear here for the first time, together with some marginal details (Plates 8—20).

According to the inscriptions in Jahangir's handwriting, the album was completed between 1608 and 1614, and was assembled (probably in collaboration with other painters) by Balchand and Govardhan. Some of the inserted miniatures are probably of an earlier date and originated in Akbar's time. Most of the miniatures are by the famous names of Akbar's *ateliers* — Aka Riza, Ustad Mansur, Farrukh Beg, Bishndas, Abul Hasan, Manohar, and others. European engravings are also glued in — copies by Dutch mannerists after Dürer, Rottenhammer and Beham. These engravings were presented to the Mughal Emperor by Jesuit missionaries from Goa. The glued-in calligraphies are three parts the work of the 16th century Persian callighrapher, Mir Ali, and the remainder by Sultan Ali Mashhadi, Muhammad Hasain, Abdur Rahim, and others. (see Baquir Mohammad, 'Muraqqa-Gulshan', *Journal of the Pakistan Historical Society*, *Vol. V, fasc. 3*, Karachi, 1957, pp. 158—161).

10. Prince Salim with a Cup of Wine and a Hound. Folio from

Jahangir's Album. Size 420 by 265 mm, including golden flower-tendril margin. The miniature enlarged by re-touching when inserted. Above, two glued-in European engravings. Náprstek Museum, Prague.

This picture is evidently a paraphrase of the Persian portraits of Shah Tahmasp's era. We know that Prince Salim (the later Emperor Jahangir) strengthened his claims to the throne by rallying the Persian aristocracy to his support while his father, Akbar, was still alive. He would be able to rely particularly on those families which had left Shah Tahmasp's court with Humayun. At this time, also he himself wore Persian garments (see the picture of Salim and his religious patron, Sheikh Salim Chishti in the Staatliches Museum, Berlin, reproduced by Kühnel in *Miniaturmalerei im islamischen Orient*, Plate 103). In this miniature, Salim is portrayed with the symbols of his two passions — wine and hunting.

Jahangir writes in his memoirs, that as a mere prince, he employed the painter, Aka Riza, who came from Herat. The composition of the present portrait resembles that of another picture, in the Boston Museum, signed by this artist, as well as that of other miniatures attributed to him by Coomaraswamy. (See the *Catalogue of Indian Collections in the Museum of Fine Arts, Boston, Part VI, Mughal Painting*, Cambridge, 1930, pp. 30—31; also the same subject in *Artibus Asiae*, p. 204 ff.). In this picture we also find all the characteristics of Aka Riza's personal style described by E. Schroeder in an analysis of the portrait in the Fogg Art Museum, Washington. This is almost a counterpart of the present picture. (E. Schroeder, *Persian Miniatures in the Collection of the Fogg Art Museum*, Cambridge, 1940, pp. 110 to 111, Plate 19).

75

11. Bijapur. Detail of landscape from Plate 8.

12. Courtiers Listening to Adil Shah's Music. Detail from Plate 8.

13. Ibrahim Adil Shah II. Detail from Plate 8.

14. The Musician's Hand. Detail from Plate 8.

15. Prince Salim (?). Detail from Plate 10.

16. The Diamond-Cutter. Figure from margin. Reverse of the sheet reproduced in Plate 8.

17. Flowers and a Bird. From the caption to Mir Ali's calligraphy, glued to the reverse of the same sheet.

18. An Astrologer. Figure from margin. Reverse of the same sheet.

19. Phoenix (Simurgh). Detail from margin. Obverse of the same sheet.
   With regard to the iconography of this imaginary bird, see Coomaraswamy, *op. cit.*, pp. 90—93.

20. A Lion and Birds. Detail from margin. Obverse of the same sheet.

21. Portraits of Four Mughal Courtiers in the Garden. Sheet from Jahangir's (Golshan's) Album with Sultan Ali Mashhadi's calligraphy on the reverse, and with illuminated margins. Size 420 by 265 mm. Teheran Imperial Library. C. 1600—1605.
   For comments on this album see under 9. None of the courtiers here (all of them young) is identifiable with any of the known officials of Jahangir who appear in paintings

76

of durbar scenes between the years 1615 and 1625. The setting, too, of the group portrait is unusual and, for this period, improbable. The Persian perspective of the background (the gardens) suggests the influence of one of the Persian painters employed by Salim. The figures, however, seem to be the work of a Hindu painter.

22. *Dedication of a Book. Sheet from the same album. Size 420 by 265 mm. On the reverse, Mir Ali's calligraphy and margin with horsemen. Teheran Imperial Library. C. 1600.*

The dedication of a book is a common subject in Persian and Mughal miniatures. This particular painting may refer to the history of the manuscript for which the miniature was intended (an example of this is the painting where Amir Khusrav Dihlavi dedicates his novel, *Khamse*, to his patron, the Sultan of Delhi. See Arnold-Grohman: *The Islamic Book*, 1929, Plates 84 and 85), or it may be the record of an actual event at young Prince Salim's court.

23. *The Prince Enjoying a View of Maidens Bathing. Sheet from the same album. Signed in the lower right-hand corner: 'Aka Riza Musavvir, Jahangir's slave'. Size 420 by 265 mm with margin. On the reverse, Mir Ali's calligraphy and illuminated margin. Teheran Imperial Library. C. 1608.*

Signed works of this painter are rare (see bibliography under 10). The style of the work bears out Coomaraswamy's theory that Aka Riza, alias Murid, is identical with Muhammad Riza of Meshhed, the disciple of the Persian painter, Mir Sayyid.

24. *Military Camp. Sheet from the same album. Size 420 by 265 mm.*

77

with margins. On the reverse, Mir Ali's calligraphy and illuminated margins. Teheran Imperial Library. C. 1600.

This work closely resembles Basawan's illustrations to the *Akbar-nama* (see Bibliography under 4.).

25. Feeding an Elephant. Detail from Plate 24.

26. Watering of Horses. Detail from Plate 24.

27. Hunter. Detail from the margin in Plate 24.

28. Falconer. Detail from the margin of the reverse of sheet, Plate 23.

29. Courtship. Detail from the margin of the reverse of sheet, Plate 21.

30. Falconer on Horseback. Detail from the margin of the reverse of sheet, Plate 22.

31. Madonna and Donors. Detail from the lower part of the sheet from the same album as Plates 21—24. The whole picture is composed of four small miniatures glued together. Size 420 by 265 mm with margins. On the reverse, Mir Ali's calligraphy and illuminated margins. Teheran Imperial Library. C. 1610.

This picture of the Madonna is copied, like so many other miniatures of Jahangir's reign, from a European picture, presented by Jesuit missionaries.

32. Mother with Child. Sheet from the same album. Size 420 by 265 mm. On the reverse, Mir Ali's calligraphy and illuminated margins. Teheran Imperial Library. C. 1610.

This miniature is after an Italian original of the Madonna

and Child. The miniature in the Boston Museum (signed Muhammad Mirza Al-Hasani) was painted from the same model, or from a tracing made from this miniature (see Catalogue cited, Plate 39 and elsewhere). In this case, however, the couch with the Madonna is placed in the landscape and reversed, mirror-fashion.

33. Portrait of a Poet. Loose sheet. Size 130 by 850 mm. Teheran Archaeological Museum. C. 1600. Margin of a later date.

34. The Emperor Shah Jahan on Horseback. Loose sheet. Size 245 by 145 mm. Fort Museum, Red Fort, Delhi. Second part of 17th century, after a portrait from c. 1627.

The original portrait of Shah Jahan was painted by Go-vardhan, probably round about the year, 1627, with a different landscape background and different figures (see Goetz, *Geschichte der indischen Miniaturmalerei*, Berlin, 1934, Fig. 15, from the Sotheby's auction, London, 1929.) The copyist has, on the whole, kept exactly to the original figure and part of the background (the small angels), probably following the tracing; the remaining part is his own composition. Judging by the Hindu aristocrat saluting the Emperor, this version could not have been painted before the middle of the 17th century. Shah Jahan in this youthful likeness with a beard appears in miniatures from the year 1622, the year of his revolt against his father, Jahangir, and then not again until he ascended the throne in 1627.

35. The Learned Physician, Platon Marfayant. Loose sheet. Size 206 by 105 mm. Detail. In the upper margin: the inscription, 'Portrait of Aflatun al Marfayani, scholar in medicine'. In the lower margin, the

79

*Inscription, 'The portrait was painted in 1038' (1628—1629 A.D.)
National Gallery, Prague.*

This painting is reminiscent of Persian works of the Shah
Abbas era. Nevertheless, some of the detail (a different
angle of viewpoint of the mouth and the eyes) suggests an
Indian origin, as does the fact that this miniature was
inserted in a Ragmala album (illustrations of musical modes)
painted in Rajasthan.

*36. Young Girl with Letter. Loose sheet. Size 130 by 42 mm.
Signature on margin of Rahim Dakni. Teheran Imperial Library.
Second part of 17th century.*

The name, Rahim Dakni, appears on several miniatures of
the latter part of the 17th century (see *Indian Art*, ed. Sir R.
Winstedt, London, 1947, Plate 14.) This miniature is,
however, somewhat uncharacteristic and resembles more in
style the works of the middle part of the century. Although
it bears resemblances to the work of the Deccani schools,
it is not far away, however, from the Mughal style. It is
quite possible that Rahim Dakni in fact came from the
Deccan but did not work there.

*37. Young Girl with Loosened Hair. Loose sheet. Size 107 by 57 mm.
Thick cardboard with margin encrusted with gilded ornamentation.
Glued to the reverse, a calligraphy by the 17th century Persian callig-
rapher, Muhammad Khan. Second half of the 17th century. National
Gallery, Prague.*

The stylization of the drapery points to the Deccani school;
no similar miniature, however, of Deccani origin is known.
The execution of the work places it close to the picture
'Princess' in the National Museum of India. (See catalogue,

5000 Years Art from India, Essen-Bredeney, 1959, No. 360a).

38. Young Girl with Loosened Hair. Detail from the preceding plate.
Here, the virtuosity in the painting of the hair and the
transparent Dacca muslin is plainly visible, as well as the
delicate modelling, the softness of the hands, and the neat
foreshortening of the hand in its unconventional gesture.

39. Camel Fight. Loose sheet. Size 95 by 158 mm. Teheran Archaeo-
logical Museum. Second part of 17th century.
Watching fights between animals, such as elephants, bulls
and camels, was, from time immemorial, a favourite pastime
of the Indian kings, and the Mughal Emperors kept up the
tradition. The Mughal miniaturists most frequently painted
fights between camels. A masterpiece in this genre is the
sheet in the Prince of Wales Museum, Bombay, the author-
ship of which is attributed by Khandalawala to Nanha.
(See *Mughal Miniatures*, Lalit Kala Akadami, New Delhi,
1955, Plate 5.).

40. Three Women with Fireworks. Loose sheet. Size 165 by 119 mm.
Teheran Imperial Library. C. 1640.

41. Dara Shikoh, Shah Jahan's Eldest Son, with His Armies. Loose
sheet. Size 305 by 222 mm. Fort Museum, Red Fort, Delhi. Copy
from the second part of the 18th century.
Dara Shikoh, although an erudite scholar, writer and
translator, was apparently less effective as Commander-in-
Chief of the armies than his younger brother, Aurangzib.
In the struggle for the succession which broke out between
the four brothers while Shah Jahan was still alive, Dara

81

Shikoh was unable to make good his legitimate claim to the throne, and he was defeated and executed in 1659. The original painting from which this copy was made, was probably painted around 1655, as was a similar miniature in the Museum für Völkerkunde, Berlin. (See Sattar Kheiri, *Indische Miniaturen*, Berlin, no date, Plate 14).

42. Mughal Warriors. Detail of the preceding miniature.

43. Portrait of a Young Girl with a Flower. Loose sheet. Size 177 by 110 mm. Teheran Archaeological Museum. End of the 17th century.
The designation, 'Jahangir', marked on the sheet by a Hindu scribe, is at variance with the style of the miniature. This drawing could certainly not have been made before the end of the 17th century.

44. Lovers. Drawing mounted with various calligraphies on a common sheet. Size 140 by 70 mm. Teheran Imperial Library. C. 1710.
From the likeness of the man, it may be deduced that this is a painting of Buhadur Shah (1707—1712). The drawing was probably made in the first decade of the 18th century. It seems that the painter made use of an earlier model, for some details of the configuration of the lovers bear a striking resemblance to the well-known doubleportrait of Jahangir and Nur Jahan in the Demotte Collection, Paris. (See Stchoukine, 'Portraits of Moghols, Part II', *Revue des Arts Asiatiques, Vol. VII, Part III*, Paris, 1931, Plate 56).

45. Young Girl with Lamp. Detail from a loose sheet. Size 202 by 140 mm. Prince of Wales Museum, Bombay. C. 1720.

This is a Mughal version of a common Rajput theme —
a girl on her way to keep a nocturnal tryst.

*46. Young Girls at the Holi Festival. Drawing. Size 206 by 120 mm.
National Gallery, Prague. Beginning of the 18th century.*
The Hindu Spring festival — Holi — was evidently also
celebrated at the Mughal court and often appears in miniatures. The drawing is reminiscent of another, of a group
of women, in Gagendranath Thakur's Collection. (See
Coomaraswamy, *Indian Drawings*, Plate 16).

*47. Laila Visits Majnun in the Desert. Loose sheet with calligraphies
in the margin. Teheran Archaeological Museum. First half of the
18th century.*
The well-known love-story of Laila and Majnun, set to verse
by many Persian poets, was illustrated at the Mughal court
under Akbar. (See Bodleian Picture Books, *Mughal Miniatures
of the Earlier Periods*, Oxford, 1953, Plates 1—7). This
miniature, however, was probably not painted from an
Akbar model. The tracing used by the painter, however,
probably dates from an earlier period. A painting of the
same subject in the Staatliches Museum, Berlin, identical
in composition as well as in several details, seems to be from
the 17th century. (See E. Kühnel, *Miniaturmalerei im islamischen Orient*, Plate 130).

*48. The Prince at the Lotus Lake. A sheet mounted between callig-
raphies. Size 146 by 105 mm. Teheran Imperial Library. First
part of the 18th century.*

49. *Nadre Banu with Fireworks. Loose sheet with illuminated margins. Size 175 by 212 mm. Teheran Imperial Library. First part of the 18th century.*

50. *Nocturnal Lovers' Tryst. Loose sheet. Size 145 by 120 mm. Fort Museum, Red Fort, Delhi. Second part of the 18th century.*

51. *Lovers. Detail from preceding sheet.*

ILLUSTRATIONS IN THE TEXT

I. Genghis Khan Prays for Victory in the Kipchat Desert. P. 251 of the illustrated manuscript of the History of the Mongols (see Plates 2—5).

II. After his Victory over Iran and Turan, Aghur Gives Orders for a Severe Fast. Upper part of another sheet from the same manuscript. Painter, Basawan.

III. A Feast with Music and Dancers. Detail of a further sheet from the same manuscript.

IV. The Princess Aroused from Sleep by Burglars. Detail of the sheet, Plate 6.

V. Islamic Scholar. Detail of margin. Reverse of sheet, Plate 24.

VI. Islamic Scholar. Detail of margin. Same sheet.

VII. Falconry. Detail of margin. Reverse of the sheet, Plate 22.

VIII. Muhammad Khan's Calligraphy. Reverse of the sheet, Plate 37.

IX. Rajput Officer of Shah Jahan. Detail from miniature, Plate 34.

X. Maidservant. Detail from miniature, Plate 50.

85

SHORT BIBLIOGRAPHY

Arnold T. V.: *Painting in Islam*, Oxford 1929

Arnold T. V. and Binyon L.: *The Court Painters of the Grand Moguls*, Oxford 1921

Auboyer J.: 'Un maître Hollandais du XVIIᵉ siècle s'inspirant des miniatures Mogholes', *Arts Asiatiques*, Tome II, Fasc. 4, Paris 1955

Baquir M.: 'Muraqqa-i-Gulshan', *Pakistan Historical Society Journal*, Vol. III, Part 3, Karachi 1957

Bielowski J.: 'Malarstwo miniaturowe Indyjskie za dynastii Wielkiego Mogola', *Przeglad Orientalisticzny* Vol. III, Part 23, Warszawa 1957

Bodleian Picture Books No 9: *Mughal Miniatures of the Earlier Periods*, Oxford 1953

Brown P.: *Indian Painting under the Mughals A.D. 1500 to A.D. 1750*, Oxford 1924

Clarke St.: *Thirty Mugul Paintings of the School of Jahangir*, Victoria and Albert Museum Portfolios, London 1922

Coomaraswamy A. K.: *Catalogue of the Indian Collections of the Museum of Fine Arts*, Boston, Part VI 'Mughal Painting', Boston 1930

Coomaraswamy A. K.: 'Mughal Portraiture', *Orientalisches Archiv*, Vol. III

Coomaraswamy A. K.: 'Notes on Mughal Painting', *Artibus Asiae*, Vol. III, 1927

Dickinson E. C.: 'The Treatment of Nature in Mughal Painting', *Pakistan Quarterly*, Vol. I, Part 6, Karachi 1959

Dimand M. S.: 'An Exhibition of Islamic and Indian Painting', *Metropolitan Museum of Art Bulletin*, Vol. XIV, New York 1955

Dimand M. S.: 'Mughal Painting under Akbar the Great'. *Ibid.*, Vol. XII, New York 1953

Dimand M. S.: 'Several Illustrations from the Dastan-i Amir Hamza in American Collections', *Artibus Asiae*, Vol. XI, Part 1, Ascona 1948

Dimand M. S.: 'The Emperor Jahangir, connoisseur of paintings', *Metropolitan Museum of Art Bulletin*, N. S. Vol. II, New York 1944

Eastman A. C.: 'Four Mughal Emperor Portraits in the City Art Museum of St. Louis', *Journal of Near Eastern Studies*, Vol. XV, Part 2, Chicago 1956

Gangoly O. C.: *Historical Miniatures of the Jahangir School*, Roopam 1920

Goetz H.: 'Indische historische Portraits', *Asia Major*, Leipzig 1925

Goetz H.: 'Die Malschulen des Mittelalters und die Anfänge der Moghul-Malerei in India', *Ostasiatisches Zeitschrift*, N. F. Vol. III, 1926

Goetz H.: *Bilderatlas zur Kulturgeschichte Indiens in der Grossmoghul Zeit*, Berlin 1930

Goetz H.: 'Indian Miniatures in German Museum and Private Collections', *Eastern Art Quarterly*, Vol. II, Philadelphia 1930

Goetz H.: 'The Early Oudh School of Mughal Painting', *Baroda State Museum Bulletin*, Vol. IX, Part 1–2, Baroda 1952–3

Gluck H.: *Die Indische Miniaturen des Hamzae-Romanes*, Vienna 1925

86

Goddard M.: 'Les marges du Murakka Gulshan, Athai-i-Iran', *Annales du service archéologique de l'Iran*, Paris 1936
Gradmann E.: *Miniatures indiennes*, Lausane 1953
Gray B.: 'A Collection of Indian Portraits', *British Museum Quarterly*, Vol. 10, London 1935
Gray B.: 'Intermingling of Mughal and Rajput Art', *India Cultural Review*, Vol. III, No 1, Rome 1954
Sattar Kheiri: *Indische Miniaturen*, Berlin, no date
Krishnadasa R.: *Mughal Miniatures*, Lalit Kala Akadami, India, 1955
Kühnel E. and Goetz H.: *Indische Buchmalerei aus dem Jahangir Album der Staat bibliothek zu Berlin*, Bern 1924
Kühnel E.: *Indische Miniaturen aus dem Besitz der Staatlichen Museen zu Berlin*, Berlin, no date
Kühnel E.: *Moghul Malerei*, Berlin, no date
Martin F. R.: *Miniature Painting and Painters of Persia, India and Turkey*, London 1912
Metha N. C.: *Studies in Indian Painting*, Bombay 1926
Pinder-Wilson R. H.: 'Three Illustrated Manuscripts of the Mughal Period', *Ars Orientalis*, Vol. II, Washington 1957
Sarre F.: 'Rembrandts Zeichnungen nach indisch-islamischen Miniaturen', *Jahrbuch der preusischen Kunstsammlungen*, 1904
Saraswati K.: 'Birds in Moghul Art', *MARG*, Vol. II, No. 2, Bombay 1948
Skelton R.: 'The Mughal Artist Farrokh Beg', *Ars Orientalis*, Vol. II, Washington 1957
Staude W.: 'Contribution a l'étude de Basawan', *Revue des arts asiatiques*, Tome 8, Paris 1934
Staude W.: 'Les artists de la cour d'Akbar et les illustrations du Dastan i Amir Hamzae', *Arts Asiatiques*, Vol. II, Fasc. 1—2, Paris 1955
Stchoukine I.: *La Peinture Indienne de l'époque des Grands Moghols*, Paris 1929
Stchoukine I.: *Les Miniatures Indiennes de l'époque des Grand Moghols au Musée de Louvre*, Paris 1929
Stchoukine I.: 'Portraits Moghols', Part 1—4, *Revue des Arts asiatiques*, Tome VII—IX, Paris 1931—1934
Stchoukine I.: 'Un Bustan de Sadi illustré par artistes moghols', *Ibid.*, Tome XI.
Strzygowski J. und Glück H.: *Indische Miniaturen im Schlosse Schönbrunn*, Wien 1923
Tyulayev S. J. and others: *Indian Art in Soviet Collections*, Moscow 1955
Welezs E. F.: 'Mughal Painting at Burlington House', *The Burlington Magazine*, 1948
Welezs E. F.: *Akbar's Religious Thought as Reflected in Mogul Painting*, London 1952
Wilkinson J. V. S. and Binyon L.: *The Light of Canopus, Anvar-i-Suhaili*, London 1929
Wilkinson J. V. S.: *Mughal Painting*, London 1948
Wilkinson J. V. S.: 'An Indian Manuscript of the Golestan of the Shah Jahan Period', *Ars Orientalis*, Vol. II, Washington 1957

PRINTED IN CZECHOSLOVAKIA

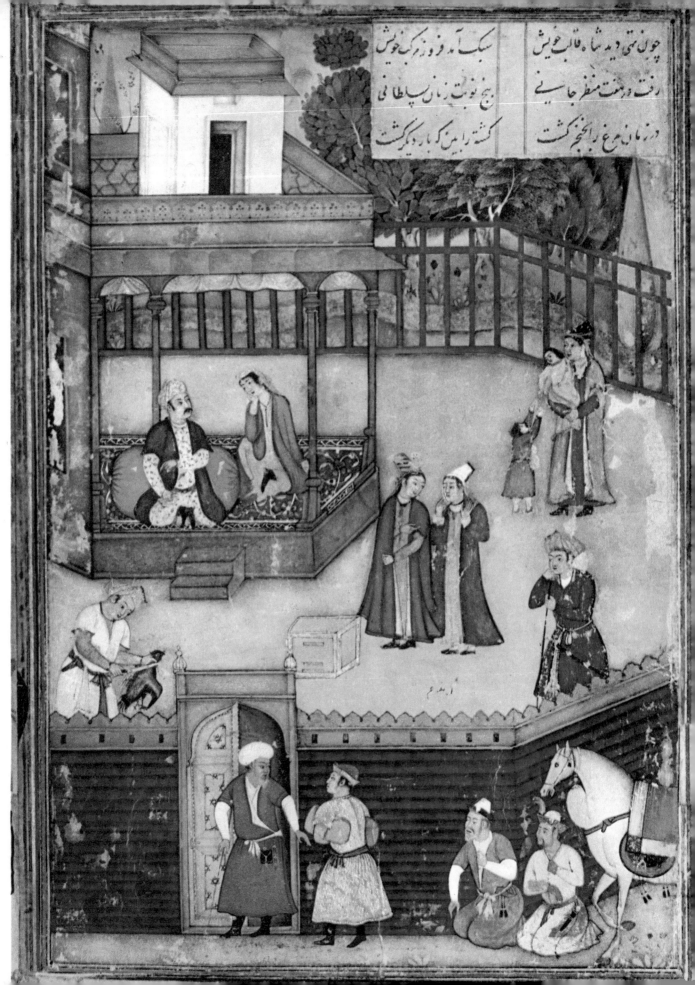

چوں نهی دید شاہ قالب خویش
سبک آمد فروز مرکب خویش

رفت و همت منظر حا سینی
بیح نوبت زمان سلطانی

در زمانی مرغ را بنخچه گشت
کشته را میں که بار دیگر گشت

کرد و داد مباد ی حصول آن مأمول منذ از رو متوالی شود بریتال صورت حال یسوکای بها در که ذات بی بعال وصدف در

دولت شبند و وصول که اکب سلطنت چنکیز خان و وازان بلاد و او روق بها ذار نبا و اخفاد و اعقاب رکوار ایشان علی الخصوص

ناصر الدین سلطان محمود غازان خان که الطناب سلطنت آبش بادا و آدطو رشه و دو مقعد دبا و افرادا مدادنصرت ا

الا می لا له الکرام علیه و علیهم الصلوة و السلام دیستان یسوکای بها در آن سه دوقسم است بربین منوال قسم اول ازید

فرزندان او و بعضی حکایات ایشان یسوکای بها در پدر چنکیز خان است و مغولان مدرا الحکیمه کویند و او با دتشاب با

یعنی عمام و غزاد کان حمله مطیع و متابع و با تفاق او را از میان خویش باد تشاب نصب کردند و بها ری دره ی دلاوی یسوکوشب

و ازکتب تواریخ که بدان اصطلاحات اقباس کنند چناک من اوله الی الآخره خواص و عوام را معلوم و مفهوم کردو نوا

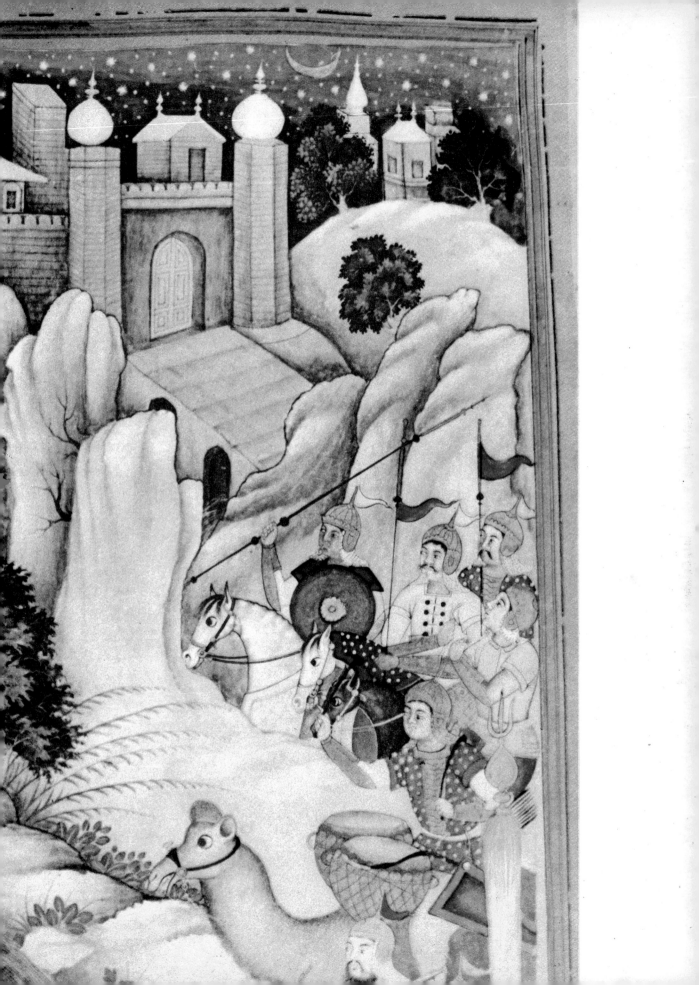

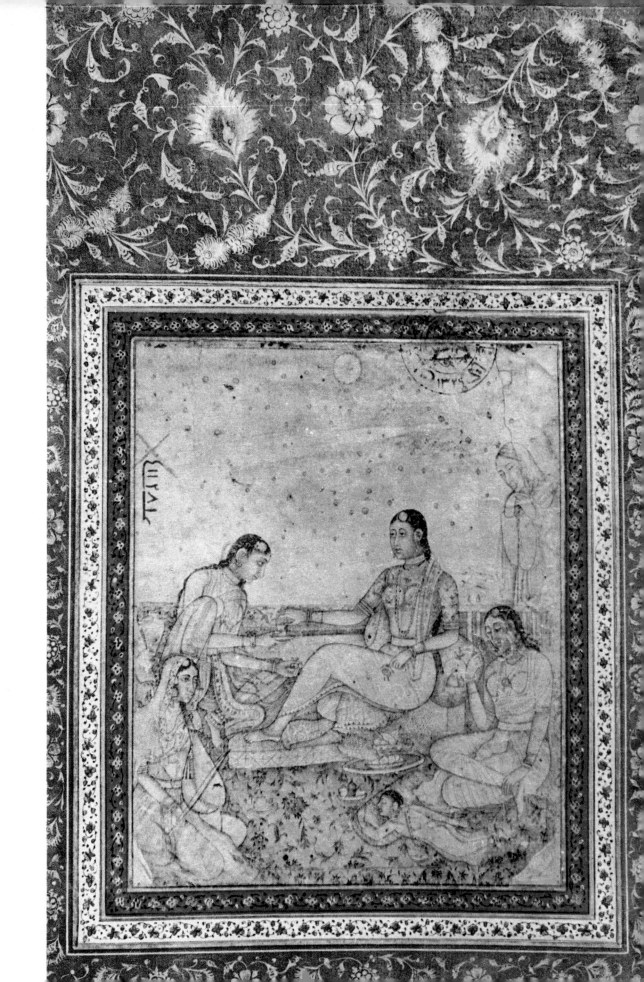

7

9

3

15

25

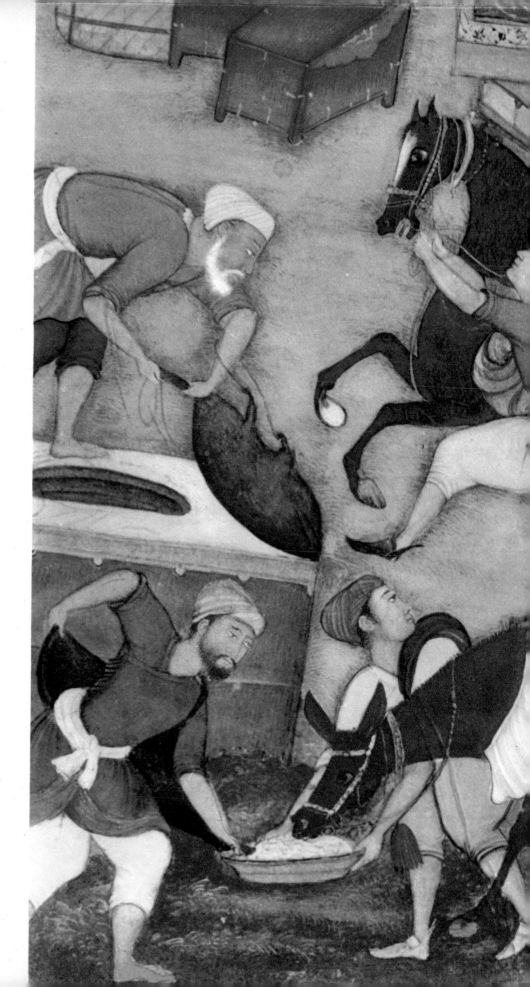

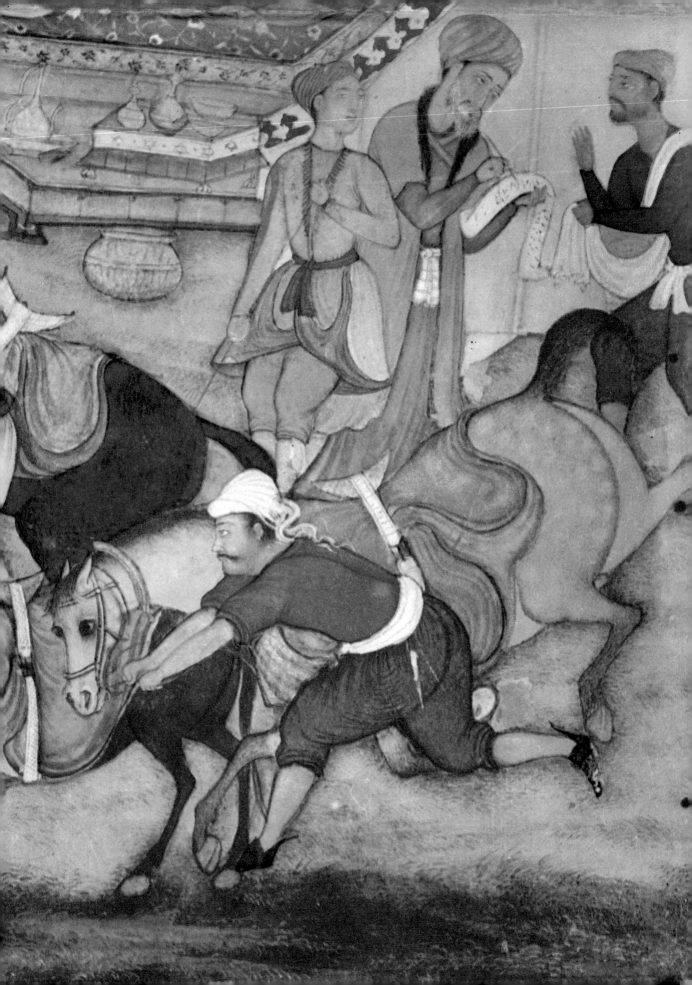

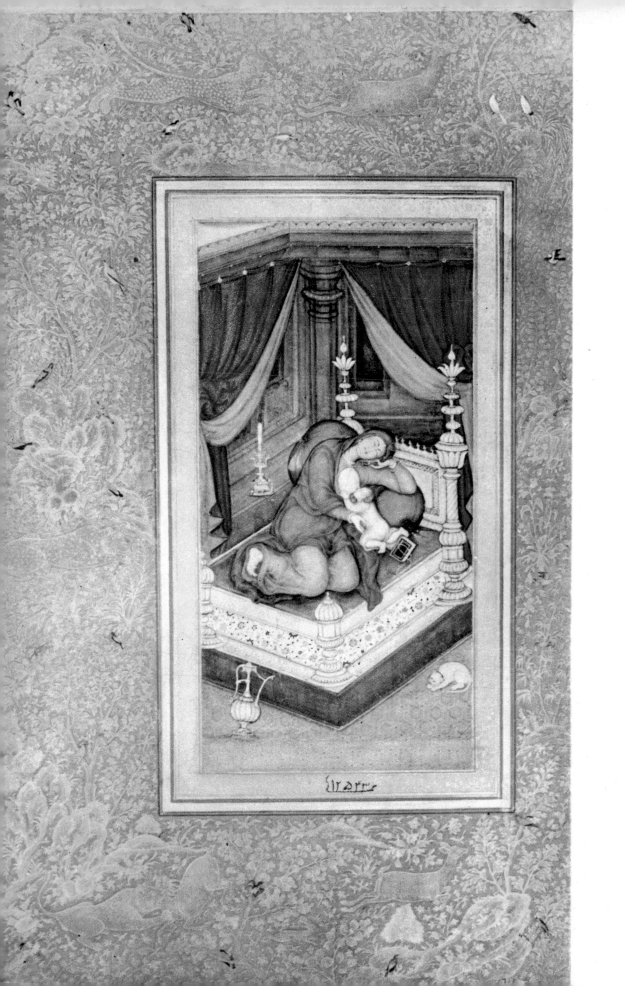

32

37

43